Flex Your Communication:
47 Tips for Every Day Success at Work

by Terra L. Fletcher

Copyright © 2019, 2026 Terra L. Fletcher

All rights reserved.

ISBN: 978-1-0953-0671-0

To my husband, Andrew Fletcher,
who has seen the best and the worst
of my communication, loves me anyway,
and continues with me on the journey
of becoming better human beings

TABLE OF CONTENTS

DISCLAIMER vii
PREFACE 8
Introduction 10
Section 1: Ace the First Meet 11
Chapter 1. Never Be Awkward Again 12
Chapter 2. Ask Better Questions 17
Chapter 3. Don't Ask *This* Question 22
Chapter 4. Dress Up! 25
Chapter 5. Listen UP! 29
Section 2: Follow Up with Flair 33
Chapter 6. Ace Follow-Up and Keep Connected 34
Chapter 7. Write Personal Notes 37
Chapter 8. Talk Their Way 40
Section 3: Everyday Communication 44
Chapter 9. Know the Types of Communication 45
Chapter 10. Watch Your Nonverbals 48
Chapter 11. Understand Four Communication Styles 52
Chapter 12. Be Concise 59
Chapter 13. Give Effective Feedback 62
Chapter 14. Take Feedback and Criticism 66
Chapter 15. Give Professional Compliments 70
Chapter 16. Accept Compliments 73
Chapter 17. Know When and How to Say No 76

Section 4: Digital Communication 79
Chapter 18. Keep Up with Technology 80
Chapter 19. Use Social Media Like A Pro 83
Section 5: Communicate Across Cultures 87
Chapter 20. Communicate Across Cultures 88
Section 6: Communicate with Any Generation 91
Chapter 21. Overcome Generational Myopia 92
Chapter 22. Work Well with Traditionals 95
Chapter 23. Work Well with Baby Boomers 99
Chapter 24. Work Well with Gen Xers 101
Chapter 25. Work Well with Xennials 104
Chapter 26. Work Well with Millennials 108
Chapter 27. Work Well with Gen Z 111
Chapter 28. Work Well With Gen Alpha 115
Chapter 29. Be an Effective New Leader 119
Section 7: Gender-Inclusive Communication 123
Chapter 30. Communicate Beyond Gender Stereotypes .. 124
Chapter 31. Communicate Inclusively Across Genders 129
Section 8: Leadership Level Communication 132
Chapter 32. First, Know Thyself 133
Chapter 33. Hold Others Accountable 137
Chapter 34. Flex Your Style 141
Chapter 35. Create a Safe and Healthy Workplace 144
Chapter 36. Show Appreciation on THEIR Terms 148
Chapter 37. Encourage Brand Advocacy 152

Section 9: Persuasive Communication 155

Chapter 38. Get People to say, "Yes!" 156

Chapter 39. Communicate Consultatively 160

Chapter 40. Empower Through Communication 164

Section 10: Communication Breakdowns 168

Chapter 41. Manage Conflict 169

Chapter 42. Confront With Clarity 172

Chapter 43. Work Productively with Difficult People 177

Section 11: Next Level Communication 181

Chapter 44. Keep Yourself Motivated 182

Chapter 45. Motivate Others 187

Chapter 46. Get Out of Your Comfort Zone 191

Chapter 47. Make Long-Term Change 195

A Final Word 199

Acknowledgments 201

About the Author 202

DISCLAIMER

I teach communication, *and* I still get it wrong sometimes. I continue to learn, stay engaged with the world around me, and work to become a better communicator.

Not every idea in this book will apply to every situation. Use your judgment. Take what resonates, adapt what doesn't, and leave what isn't useful.

The goal of this book is to educate, inspire, and entertain while encouraging more thoughtful, intentional communication.

Keep learning. Keep observing. Keep choosing how you show up.

PREFACE

For almost two decades, organizations have come to me believing that a marketing campaign would solve their internal challenges. It rarely does.

In my consulting work, I consistently uncover deeper issues: reduced sales, high employee turnover, reputational damage, and stalled growth. These problems aren't caused by poor marketing. They're often rooted in how people communicate *inside* the organization.

I wrote this book to address that root issue. **When communication improves, reputation follows. Morale rises. Production and visibility increase. At that point, marketing becomes more effective and easier.**

Marketing and communication have always fascinated me. I studied relentlessly and learned from real people. Many students, executives, employees, and experts were willing to share what worked and what didn't.

I speak at schools, conferences, and various businesses. After a twenty-minute talk or even a two-day speaking engagement, I still have more to say. I wrote this book for those who come up to me after a session with more questions. It's for those eager to explore communication in depth. It's for those who are ready and willing to flex their communication and find more success at work every day.

INTRODUCTION

Most professionals can improve their listening, clarity, and conflict management. **Communication is a skill, and like any skill, it improves with awareness, intention, and practice.**

This book is written for professionals who are willing to examine their habits, make adjustments, and see measurable improvement over time.

The chapters are designed to be practical and approachable. You can read them in order or jump to what's most relevant right now. Many leaders also use the concepts as discussion topics for team meetings.

Use this book actively. Mark it up. Revisit sections. Please apply what you learn and talk about it with others because communication doesn't improve in isolation.

If you want better results at work, this is a place to start.

SECTION 1: ACE THE FIRST MEET

CHAPTER 1. NEVER BE AWKWARD AGAIN

I often feel like 15-year-old me, all dressed up for a wedding. My hair professionally done, wearing my best friend's Wonderbra and four-inch heels. We were strutting through the mall between the ceremony and reception when I fell flat on my face. That's when I remembered I wasn't the polished person I was pretending to be. I was just an awkward teenager.

That awkward, clumsy feeling still shows up sometimes, especially at networking events. I can feel out of place, uncomfortable, and just plain shy. The difference now is that I know how to work through it. And if I can do that, you can too.

Often, to get what you want, you need to flex your communication and adapt your natural style. In this book, we'll work on communication and self-presentation together. Whether it's a networking event, conference, virtual meeting, or social occasion, these tips will help you make a stronger first impression and convey the message you set out to convey.

Before You Network

Take a few practical steps to feel more comfortable. Eat a small snack beforehand. Brush your teeth. (If eating makes you more self-conscious around people you don't know, it's reasonable to skip food at networking events unless a sit-down meal is part of the program.)

Be mindful of caffeine. For some people, caffeine combined with adrenaline can lead to fidgeting or shaking.

If you tend to spill food or drinks, avoid white. A white dress and red tea? Guaranteed to spill. (Or is that just me?)

Wear something professional that instills confidence. Black or navy covers many sins. I like a sheath dress, one piece means no coordinating required. Gentlemen, check out RealMenRealStyle.com for guidance on attire.

If wearing a nametag, place it on your right side. Check your appearance in a full-length mirror and give yourself a quick pep talk. Bonus points if you say it out loud.

Stand Up Straight

Posture has been referred to as a leading barometer of success. The way you look and move contributes significantly to first impressions. Walk into the room with your head up, a confident smile, and a direct gaze. Stand tall with your ears, shoulders, hips, knees, and ankles aligned.

In virtual settings, the same principle applies: sit upright, face the camera, and avoid distracting movements.

Invite Conversation

If you're more reserved, make it easier for people to approach you. Wear or display something distinctive that invites comment, such as a unique piece of jewelry, a bold tie, or a well-designed name badge.

When someone approaches, don't just turn your head. Turn your whole body toward them and reward their effort with your full attention. If you're in a group, take a small step back to make space. Offer a firm handshake when appropriate and smile. In virtual or hybrid settings, acknowledge people by name and respond visibly and verbally.

Feeling bold? Seek out conversations by noticing others' artifacts. A golf pin. A school ring. A background item on a video call. There's your opener. "I couldn't help but notice your…"

Ace Small Talk

Before attending an event, listen to the news or read something interesting. Prepare one or two conversation-ready ideas or questions, always keeping your audience in mind. A room of accountants might appreciate a question about the newest tax law. At a human resources event, ask about recruitment strategies or social media success. This preparation matters just as much for virtual meetings, where awkward silences can feel amplified.

Consider what you might be asked. "What's new?" comes up often. Prepare a brief response about a current project, family update, or upcoming trip.

If you're meeting many new people, expect "Where are you from?" or "What do you do?" Find an interesting detail to extend the conversation beyond a one-word answer.

I might say, "I'm from Shawano, about 35 miles from Green Bay. Shawano County is the Barn Quilt Capital of Wisconsin and home to Sun Drop, the golden cola."

The First Words

Nearly any subject is fair game. It is okay to begin with the weather, the food, or the atmosphere. But keep it positive!

What matters most isn't the topic, but the tone. Skilled communicators pay attention to conversational cues. Are people focused on relationships or tasks? People or projects? Adjust accordingly.

If there's an influencer you'd like to meet, approach the event organizer for an introduction. When introducing others, include an interesting detail. "This is Sheila. She loves canoeing and has a Labrador that plays fetch until exhaustion."

Choose Your Seat

Where you sit influences the professional value you gain from an event. If your goal is to meet new people, avoid sitting with those you already know. At lectures, sit up front. You'll hear better, stay engaged, and be more likely to participate.

At meals, choose a nearly full table when possible. Save your seat as you mingle. Be intentional. Who here might connect you with a future opportunity?

Keep It Going

If a conversation stalls, change the topic. "By the way…" works well. If body language suggests it's time to move on, don't overstay. Thank them and mention you want to catch someone else before leaving.

Before You Forget!

Right after an event, jot down a few notes about the people you met. Write down personal details: names, interests, family notes, anything that will help you follow up thoughtfully.

Remember Names

It's challenging, but doable. Concentrate on names. Ask again if needed. Repeat them. Make associations.

Help others remember your name by saying it clearly. I often explain that Terra has two Rs, like terra-cotta or Terra Nova. If writing, I note it's pronounced "TARE-a," not "TAR-ra."

Make sure your email and LinkedIn profiles include a recognizable photo so people can connect your name to your face.

Once the initial awkwardness fades, the real work begins. Strong communication isn't just about showing up; it's about knowing what to say next. Let's start by asking better questions.

CHAPTER 2. ASK BETTER QUESTIONS

We ask questions to understand people, clarify problems, collaborate, and lead more effectively. Asking better questions and knowing when to stay quiet strengthen every professional relationship.

Get Comfortable with Silence

Silence is golden. Allow your conversation partner the time they need to form a reply. People aren't used to being asked thoughtful questions; they're used to being told what to do.

Some of your most introspective and insightful colleagues need more time to respond. Be patient. Allow them space to volunteer information. You don't need to fill every pause.

Open Versus Closed Questions

Effective communicators flex the type of questions they ask.

Closed-ended questions can be answered briefly. They're useful for narrowing focus, guiding a very talkative person, or gaining clarity or commitment when time is limited.

Open-ended questions invite broader responses. They help uncover thoughts, motivations, and feelings, and they give the other person control over how much they share.

You don't need to memorize these; use them as prompts and adapt them naturally.

Closed-Ended Questions

- Are?
- Do?
- Who?
- When?
- Where?
- Which?

Open-Ended Questions

- How?
- Why?
- What was it like to . . .?
- What was the best part of . . .?
- What's surprised you the most about . . .?
- How did you feel about . . .?

"Getting to Know You" Questions

It's fine to start with "How are you?" or "How was your weekend?" Don't stop there. After an opening exchange, consider asking one of the following:

- How do you spend most of your time at work?
- What do you enjoy most about what you do?
- Why did you choose your profession?
- What are you currently reading or learning?

Choose one or two that feel natural. The goal is connection, not interrogation.

Questions That Can Backfire

In stressful situations, specific questions raise defenses and shut people down. Rapid-fire or leading questions can feel accusatory, even when that isn't your intent. For example:

- Why are you behind schedule?
- What's the problem?
- Who isn't keeping up?
- Don't you agree that Susan is the issue?

Questions like these often trigger fight, flight, or freeze responses. And as you can probably feel, they don't invite openness. If you want candid answers, slow down. Stay flexible. Focus on understanding before evaluation.

Don't Be Vague or Overly Broad

Questions like "Tell me about yourself" can feel overwhelming or intrusive, especially if *you* haven't shared anything in return. More reserved or private individuals may shut down.

If you sense discomfort, step back. Say, "Let me rephrase that." Move to a more focused question, listen for cues about what they want to discuss.

Questions to Empower

Thoughtful questions build trust and accountability. For example:

- To gain clarity: "Can you explain more about this situation?"

- To encourage critical thinking: "What are the consequences of this approach?"
- To expand options: "Is there another way to look at this?"
- To create ownership: "Based on your experience, what do you suggest?"

Tip for New Managers

When someone asks a question you *could* answer immediately, pause. Facilitate discussion first.

> *"That's a great question. I'm curious—has anyone else dealt with something similar? What worked or didn't?"*

You'll come across as thoughtful and inclusive, not as a know-it-all. (In my experience, the group's answer is often better than my own anyway.)

Questions to Propel Your Career

One of the most effective ways to grow is to learn directly from people you admire. When talking with someone who's where you'd like to be in a few years, consider asking:

- What advice do you wish you'd received earlier in your career?
- What book, article, or podcast has helped you recently?
- What are you most excited about right now in your work?

A strong closing question, such as "How can I support you right now?" is appropriate in many professional settings.

Questions to Ask Your Boss

Start by asking for time:

> "I'd appreciate fifteen minutes to talk about my future here and how I can continue to add value."

Then ask:

- How can I better leverage my strengths?
- What growth opportunities should I be preparing for

Now that you're asking better questions, let's make sure we don't ask this one thing.

CHAPTER 3. DON'T ASK *THIS* QUESTION

In 2010, an acquaintance asked my husband and me whether we were both working. Many had recently lost their jobs during the economic downturn. Andrew replied, "I am. She's not."

I tried not to show it, but I was crushed. I was raising our baby and a fledgling business. That moment stayed with me. It was when I decided to stop asking, "Do you work?" or "What do you do?"

In the previous chapter, we explored how asking better questions strengthens connections. This chapter focuses on one common question that often does the opposite.

"What do you do?" seems innocent enough. The problem isn't the question itself; it's the expected answer: a job title.

Why is this an issue?

1. Responding with a job title can unintentionally diminish people who don't work outside the home. Retired individuals, stay-at-home parents, caregivers, and others may feel their value is reduced. Work takes many forms, even when it isn't tied to a paycheck.

2. We often attach too much identity and worth to titles and income. When a job is lost through layoffs, transitions, or economic downturns, people can lose not just their jobs but also a sense of self.

3. A title rarely captures the whole story. If you're asked what you do for work, consider responding in a way that reflects purpose as well as position.

> For example: "I help people solve conflicts at work so they can enjoy what they do," or "I work part-time so I can spend more time with my family and volunteer."

Ask a Better Question

A simple shift changes everything. Try asking:

> "How do you spend most of your time?" or
> "What do you do for fun?"

These questions invite fuller answers and open the door to genuine conversation.

Be More Interesting

If someone asks about your education, you can list your degree, or you can share a story about the professor who shaped your thinking or the moment you realized what you wanted to study.

Read more. People who read tend to be more engaging conversationalists, not because they're smarter, but because they have more perspectives to draw from.

Try new things. Even if you don't stick with them, experiences like taking an art class or trying ice-skating give you stories, insight, and empathy.

Travel when you can. Exposure to different cultures, foods, climates, and ways of living expands how you see the world and how you connect with others.

Now that you know what to ask and what to avoid, the next step is making sure your presence supports the conversation.

How you look, move, and carry yourself sends signals long before you speak. Let's take a closer look at that next.

CHAPTER 4. DRESS UP!

We judge books by their covers. Whether that's fair or not, it's reality. You have only a few seconds to make a first impression, and much of that impression is visual.

The good news is that you have some control over it. What you wear sends signals about confidence, credibility, and self-awareness. First impressions shape how comfortable you feel and how others respond to you.

What Is Your Message?

Before choosing clothes, ask a better question: *How do I want to be perceived in this setting?* Professional? Approachable? Creative? Authoritative?

The average American spends about four percent of their annual income on clothing, *less* than what's often spent on gas or dining out. You don't need an expensive wardrobe. You need one that works for *you* and aligns with the message you want to send.

Terra's Wardrobe Recommendations

*These are mine. You get to create your own. Think of these as examples, not expectations.

1. **Neat and Clean**

Take care of your clothes. Wash them properly. Store them well. Avoid wrinkles. If something looks wrinkled on the hanger in the store, it's unlikely to improve at home. I like to squeeze and stretch fabric before buying it. How does it recover? If it doesn't, I pass. (Unless you enjoy ironing. I do not.) Be mindful when eating and drinking. Carry stain-removal wipes. Keep shoes in good repair. These small choices reduce distraction.

2. Modest

Modesty is subjective and highly contextual. What matters is respect for your audience. Are you presenting to executives? Speaking internationally? Meeting clients for the first time? Ask yourself: Do I want people focusing on my clothes or on my message?

3. Appropriate for the Environment

Appropriate changes throughout the day. I might travel, work indoors, speak publicly, volunteer outdoors, exercise, and relax, all in one day. Each environment has its own expectations.

My husband installs flooring for a living. For him, appropriate means work shoes, jeans, and a T-shirt. He avoids clothing with offensive slogans because he's working in people's homes, even when he's grouting tile, neatness and care matter.

Brand Yourself with Clothes

If you're unsure where to start, simplify. Donate what doesn't fit or doesn't make you feel good. Notice what *does*.

Some professionals choose a personal uniform. It saves time, reduces decision fatigue, and creates consistency. I wear green. I own several green suits and tops. It's practical, sustainable, and recognizable.

My LinkedIn headline begins, *"The one in green, talking values-aligned marketing."* At conferences, people often say, "You must be the speaker; you're the one in green." That recognition supports my work. It's a choice that works for me.

Colors and Industry

Colors carry meaning, but they're influenced by culture, industry, and context. Instead of viewing these as rules, think of them as a starting point.

Safe choices, navy, black, gray, and brown, work well in conservative fields. Creative industries often allow more flexibility. Color can support trust, energy, authority, or approachability depending on how it's used. If color strategy matters in your role, consider learning more or working with a consultant.

Wardrobe Must-Knows

If you do nothing else, do this: **Wear clothes that fit.**

Fit matters more than color, brand, or price. Clothes that are too tight or too loose send unintended messages. A well-fitting outfit, regardless of budget, communicates care and confidence.

If you're overwhelmed, remember this order:

Fit first. Neatness second. Context third. Style last.

Get those right, and the rest becomes optional.

When you're dressed in a way that supports your message, you stop worrying about yourself. That frees your attention to focus where it belongs, on others.

And that's where strong communication really begins, with other people. Let's listen up!

CHAPTER 5. LISTEN UP!

Listening is easy to underestimate because we do it all the time. But effective listening, the kind that builds trust, improves decisions, and strengthens relationships, takes intention.

As we've already seen, strong communication depends on presence and curiosity. Listening is where those skills are tested. It's also where most breakdowns happen.

In this chapter, we'll look at how listening works in everyday conversations and how it changes under pressure. The goal isn't perfection. It's progress.

How Do You Listen?

We retain only a small portion of what we hear. Think back to the last meeting, conference, or class you attended. What stuck, and what did you actually apply?

One way to improve retention is to assume good intent. Most people want to be understood. When you appreciate a speaker's effort and motivation, you're more likely to listen for meaning rather than delivery.

Instead of focusing on accents, word choice, or mannerisms, concentrate on the message. Listen for ideas that are new to you.

Everyday Listening

In everyday conversations, listening requires attention to direction. Notice where the conversation is headed and resist the urge to steer it elsewhere. Listen for cues about what the other person wants to discuss. Limit interruptions. Let ideas unfold.

If you're attending a discussion, panel, or meeting with opposing viewpoints, consider ahead of time what might come up. Staying current with local news, trade publications, or industry updates also supports everyday listening. The more context you have, the easier it is to stay engaged and contribute meaningfully.

Counteract Distractions

Distractions are inevitable, and they're different for everyone. What matters is recognizing what pulls your attention away and choosing how to respond.

Internal distractions might include stress, anxiety, unfinished tasks, or personal concerns. One strategy that works for many people is writing things down. Make a short list. Capture the worry. If there's no immediate emergency, decide to return to it later.

External distractions include noise, movement, or physical discomfort. When attention drifts, gently bring it back. Keeping your eyes on the speaker helps. Resist the instinct to turn toward every sound or interruption. My mom would say when something awkward happened nearby:

> *"A polite person ignores it."*

Listening Under Load

At conferences or large events, listening becomes more challenging. Attention is divided. Devices are out. Energy is limited.

What's helped me is being intentional rather than exhaustive. Take a few notes or photos, just enough to capture key ideas. Avoid multitasking to the point where you only hear fragments of what's being said.

Travel and fatigue can also affect listening. For me, being well-rested improves focus and patience. I choose the best flight times I can afford and skip alcohol. The goal is: enough energy to stay present.

Before sessions begin, preview topics and set a simple intention. What do you want to walk away with? At the end of the day, reviewing notes with a colleague can reinforce learning.

Gain More Than Trivia

Collecting interesting facts can be fun, but listening is more powerful when it leads to action.

Ask yourself: What does the speaker want me to do differently? What's one idea I could apply? Writing down even one concrete takeaway increases the likelihood that something changes as a result of what you heard.

Listen with Your Body

Listening isn't just mental; it's physical. As an introverted speaker, I especially appreciate it when an audience is engaged. Eye contact, nodding, note-taking, and thoughtful questions encourage better communication. An engaged audience creates a better experience for everyone.

At a conference in Austin, Texas, a woman maintained steady eye contact throughout my presentation. Later, she told me English wasn't her first language and that giving her full attention helped ensure she understood every word.

Here's my feedback to you: You've been building skills chapter by chapter: showing up with intention, asking better questions, and listening more effectively.

Next, we'll focus on what happens after the conversation and how to follow up to strengthen relationships and keep the momentum going.

SECTION 2: FOLLOW UP WITH FLAIR

CHAPTER 6. ACE FOLLOW-UP AND KEEP CONNECTED

By now, you've done the hard part. You showed up with intention, asked better questions, and listened well. Follow-up isn't a new skill; it's simply how good conversations continue.

Strong follow-up reinforces trust, signals respect, and keeps relationships from fading into "nice to meet you" territory. It doesn't have to be constant or complicated. It just needs to be thoughtful.

Connect Where it Makes Sense

For me, that's LinkedIn. LinkedIn is today's Rolodex. (Wow, I'm dating myself here!) Even better, it's a long-term visibility tool that helps you stay top of mind.

When you connect with someone digitally (whether it's email or social media), jog their memory. Reference where you met or what you discussed. Add a personal note or shared interest.

The goal isn't volume, it's relevance. A smaller network of meaningful connections will serve you better than hundreds of forgotten ones.

Follow Up More Personally

Thoughtful follow-up is simply listening remembered.

After speaking at the Smart Customer Service Conference, I had a great conversation with fellow speaker Colin Gold. Two weeks later, he texted to ask how this book was coming along. That small detail mattered because it showed he'd been paying attention. If someone shares a goal or challenge, consider setting a reminder to check in with them later.

If you manage many contacts, tools like spreadsheets or CRMs can help. But what matters is remembering people, not managing them.

Be Thoughtful and Helpful

If you come across an article, blog post, event, or book that would interest your connections, send a brief message. Business tips are appreciated; something that relates to their family life or hobbies may be appropriate, too, depending on how well you know them.

If you reshare posts on LinkedIn, add context. A sentence about what stood out or why it matters goes a long way. Tag thoughtfully. Credit generously.

Choose Your Key Relationships

You have limited time, energy, and attention. Being intentional about relationships isn't about ranking people; it's about sustainability.

Make a short list of people you want to stay connected with over the next year. These might be mentors, peers, collaborators, community leaders, or friends. They don't all need to generate revenue. Many of the most meaningful professional relationships offer insight, encouragement, or perspective. Ask yourself:

- How many relationships can I realistically maintain?
- What kind of connection do I want with each person?

Find your Follow-Up Rhythm

I like to schedule quarterly conversations with a few people to encourage one another, hold each other accountable, and gain perspective. Others find different rhythms work better.

I've found that setting a regular day for one-to-one meetings works well. It reduces decision fatigue and improves follow-up consistency. For in-person meetings, it reduces drive time and dining costs.

Attend Events Selectively

There are countless events. You don't need to attend all of them. Instead, consider which environments support the kinds of relationships you want to build and maintain.

Sometimes the most meaningful follow-up happens away from events altogether. A handwritten note. A thoughtful email. A quiet check-in at the right time. Those moments are often remembered the longest.

CHAPTER 7. WRITE PERSONAL NOTES

We send more messages than ever. And remember fewer of them. When was the last time you received a personal email or direct message? I mean a thoughtful, intentional one? When did you last get a real letter or even a handwritten note in your physical mailbox? Personal notes are special. We recognize the time and thought that goes into them.

Recognize a Reason

Use personal notes as a purposeful follow-up. After meeting a new connection, send a brief email or LinkedIn message that references your conversation.

Thank-you and congratulatory notes carry more weight when they're timely and thoughtful. Choose the format your audience will appreciate most: email, handwritten note, or physical mail.

Pay attention to milestones. Watch LinkedIn and business publications for achievements worth acknowledging. If someone refers you, supports a project, or goes out of their way to help, respond promptly. A handwritten note is often appropriate in this case. Consistent, specific appreciation builds trust and strengthens professional relationships.

Choose the Right Format

Handwritten notes are memorable because they're rare. They often get opened, read, and saved.

That said, handwritten isn't always practical or appropriate. Other personal options can work well when done thoughtfully:

- A short, specific email (not a template)
- A personalized LinkedIn message
- A voice memo
- A mailed note card instead of a full letter

What matters most is that the message feels considered, not automated.

Slow Down

Whether you're writing by hand or typing, slow down enough to be clear. Write deliberately. Check spelling and grammar. If it helps, draft your message first, then rewrite it more naturally. Clarity increases the likelihood that your note will be read and appreciated.

Be Personal

To make the recipient feel special, make it specific. Don't just say thank you; *tell them why* you appreciate what they did. Did their efforts in coordinating the conference make it a more enjoyable event for you?

Make Delivery Easy

Here's what's worked for me: Ask for contact information early, before you need it. That way, a note doesn't feel expected, and you're not scrambling later.

If you send something to an office, addressing it "to the attention of" the recipient can help ensure it reaches the right person. A simple "personal" or "confidential" note on the envelope can prevent it from being mistaken for junk mail.

Reduce Friction

Personal notes are easier to write when the barrier is low. I keep stamps on hand and buy bulk packs of professional-looking cards. I have a small wire basket with cards sorted by occasion. I restock whenever a section runs low.

Make it Routine

When tasks become part of our routine, they don't seem like a chore. If it works for you, put "write notes" on your calendar at a regular time each week. Jimmy Fallon does his thank-you notes on Fridays.

Personal notes work because they respect how people want to be treated: as individuals, not entries in a contact list. As you continue building relationships, the next step is learning how to tailor your communication not just to what you want to say, but to how the other person best receives it.

CHAPTER 8. TALK THEIR WAY

Have you ever worked with someone you couldn't get through to, no matter how clearly you thought you were communicating? Often, the issue isn't effort or intent. It's style.

By now, you've learned how to show up well, ask better questions, listen more effectively, and follow up with intention. This chapter connects those skills by introducing a common yet often invisible barrier: **differences in communication style**.

Here, we'll build awareness. In the next chapter, we'll dig deeper into specific styles and how to adapt more intentionally.

Communication Styles and Our Blind Spots

Communication styles are deeply ingrained. They're shaped by both heredity and environment, and for most of us, they remain relatively consistent over time. Because our own style is all we've ever known, it's easy to assume it's neutral or even "normal." That assumption creates a knowledge gap in communication style.

We Are Biased, Communication Style Biased

Communication style bias is one of the most common (and least recognized) forms of bias. It tends to surface when we encounter someone whose style is noticeably different from our own.

Introverts and extroverts often struggle to understand each other. An extrovert may jump in with ideas or possible answers, believing they're being helpful. Meanwhile, the introvert may shut down because their thought process has been interrupted. This is just one example.

Style mismatches also show up in differences around:

- Pace (fast vs. deliberate)
- Detail (big picture vs. specifics)
- Directness (blunt vs. diplomatic)
- Processing time (thinking aloud vs. reflecting quietly)

When these differences aren't recognized, frustration builds on both sides.

Overcome Communication Barriers

As with everything else in this book, awareness comes first. Understanding your own communication style and recognizing that others experience the world differently lays the groundwork for healthier relationships. **Skilled communicators don't abandon their natural style; they learn when and how to flex it.**

Flexibility isn't about changing who you are. It's about increasing the likelihood that your message is received as intended.

Choose Their Medium

Different messages call for different channels, and different people respond better to different mediums.

Some teams prefer quick texts for last-minute updates. Others need face-to-face conversations for complex or sensitive topics.

Still others want time to process information before responding. (That's me!)

Matching the medium to both the message and the person improves clarity and reduces friction. This doesn't mean you accommodate every preference all the time, but it does mean being thoughtful about when flexibility will lead to better outcomes.

Be Clear and Concise

Clear communication respects people's time and attention.

Whether speaking or writing, concise messages reduce confusion and increase follow-through. Preparing your thoughts in advance, eliminating filler, and proofreading important messages all contribute to clarity.

Be Approachable

Accessibility sends a powerful signal. Being available, physically or psychologically, encourages communication before minor issues become larger ones. When someone brings you a concern or question, a simple "thank you for telling me" keeps the door open.

Listening doesn't require immediate agreement. You can acknowledge someone's perspective without endorsing it. Appreciation and boundaries can and should coexist.

Listening Is Not Agreement

Listening fully doesn't mean surrendering judgment or avoiding decisions.

It means gathering enough information to respond wisely. When people feel heard, they're more likely to accept feedback, even if it isn't what they hoped for.

Where This Leads

We've already touched on the reality that people communicate differently. This chapter names the friction that creates.

Next, we'll look more closely at common communication styles and practical ways to adapt without losing authenticity or authority.

Understanding *how* people communicate is what allows all the skills you've built so far to work together.

SECTION 3: EVERYDAY COMMUNICATION

CHAPTER 9. KNOW THE TYPES OF COMMUNICATION

Communication is dynamic (ever-changing) and systemic (it occurs in systems). It has two levels of meaning: relationship and context. Communication is influenced by how we feel, the environment we're in, and even the time of day. All aspects of communication are intertwined.

At a high level, communication consists of three primary segments: verbal, nonverbal, and paraverbal. Understanding these categories gives you a clearer picture of what's happening in any interaction, even when something feels "off," but you can't quite name why.

Verbal Communication

Verbal communication is the content of what we say or write, the actual words used. Language evolves, sometimes faster than we'd like. (The word literally, much to my dismay, now means both literally and figuratively.)

Our word choices often change based on the system we're in. The way we speak in a board meeting differs from how we talk with friends. Clarity improves when we choose words intentionally and adjust them to the context.

Nonverbal Communication

Nonverbal communication refers to how we use our bodies, posture, movement, facial expression, proximity, and physical presence. We are constantly communicating nonverbally, whether we intend to or not.

Context matters. The nonverbals that work in a one-on-one conversation won't look the same when addressing a group or navigating a tense situation. Because nonverbal cues carry so much meaning, they deserve focused attention, which we'll explore in the next chapter.

Paraverbal Communication

Paraverbal communication is how we say what we say. Tone, pace, volume, pauses, and emphasis shape how a message is received. Listeners often decide whether someone sounds confident, uncertain, impatient, or engaged before fully processing the words themselves.

Communication Mediums

In organizational settings, communication typically falls into two media categories: physical and mechanical. Before choosing a medium, clarify your desired outcome.

Physical media includes anything seen and heard in real time, such as face-to-face conversations, meetings, presentations, and video conferences. Large gatherings work well for sharing a strategy or vision. Smaller meetings are better for collaboration, problem-solving, and project updates.

Mechanical media includes written and electronic communication such as email, newsletters, memos, intranet, text messages, and social media. These channels can be efficient but are more open to interpretation.

Email is best for simple messages with low risk of misunderstanding. Keep messages concise and scannable. I use bullet points and highlighting to make the key information easy to find. Emails often reinforce decisions already made in meetings, especially in U.S. workplaces.

Individual letters or notes are well-suited for recognizing extraordinary contributions. Text messaging is increasingly common for quick updates. Social media may support collaboration, morale, or internal communication through private groups or channels.

Understanding these categories helps you choose more intentionally. Skill comes from noticing how they work together in real situations.

Now that we've outlined the communication types, let's focus on the one people underestimate most and often misread: nonverbal communication.

CHAPTER 10. WATCH YOUR NONVERBALS

Nonverbal communication is always happening, whether we're aware of it or not. Our posture, expressions, gestures, and voice all send signals that shape how our message is received.

Professionalism doesn't start with perfect body language. It begins with intention, respect for the people we're communicating with, and awareness of how we show up. When nonverbal cues don't align with our message, others may read confusion, distance, or uncertainty, even when none is intended. This chapter is about noticing what you're already communicating.

Body Language Basics

Our bodies often reveal what we're feeling before our words do. Some common patterns worth noticing:

- Arms crossed may be comfortable for some people, but in some contexts can read as closed or guarded.
- Hands on hips can signal authority or feel parental.
- Hands clasped in front may suggest hesitation or self-protection.
- Hands hidden in pockets can suggest nervousness.

None of these cues is inherently good or bad. Context, culture, personality, and baseline behavior matter more than any single gesture. What's most useful to observe is the **change from someone's norm**.

Gestures also communicate emotion. Open hands tend to feel more inviting. Pointing may feel accusatory. Excessive pacing, rocking, or shifting weight can signal nervous energy, especially in high-stakes situations.

When standing, a balanced posture with feet grounded and shoulders relaxed often reads as present and confident.

Facial Expressions

Facial expressions are among the most powerful nonverbal signals. Raised eyebrows may communicate curiosity or surprise. A furrowed brow may signal concern or disagreement. A neutral expression can be interpreted many ways depending on culture and context.

Some people are naturally expressive. Others have a "resting face" that doesn't reflect how they actually feel. Rather than trying to change your face, focus on matching your expression to your intent.

Eye contact norms vary widely. In many cultures, steady eye contact signals engagement; in others, it may feel intrusive. Observe how others communicate and adjust as needed.

Space, Position, and Environment

Distance matters. Think of the close-talker on *Seinfeld*. Do you step back or forward when someone moves closer? Power dynamics, relationships, and culture all influence personal space.

Positioning in a room also communicates status and intent. Sitting at the head of a table, choosing a seat next to leadership, or placing objects between yourself and others can signal authority, defensiveness, or alignment.

Clothing and Personal Artifacts

Appearance communicates before words do. Neat or untidy. Casual or formal. Warm or cool colors. Personal artifacts, including our technology, water bottles, and notebooks, also send signals. Industry norms and organizational culture shape how expressive we can be. The goal isn't conformity. It's alignment with context.

Use Your Voice Intentionally

Your voice carries meaning beyond the words themselves. Tone, pace, volume, and pauses influence how your message lands.

Clarity matters more than correctness. Accents and regional speech patterns aren't flaws, but being understood by a diverse audience sometimes requires slowing down or enunciating more carefully.

In the part of Wisconsin where I live, I hear a lot of "and that," "ain so," and "you know what I mean?" Recording yourself or asking someone you trust to observe your patterns can help you notice habits like filler words or rushed pacing.

Think First. Slow Down.

When possible, organize your thoughts before speaking. Slowing down supports understanding for both you and your listener. Pauses give ideas time to land and create space for others to contribute.

People process information differently. A measured pace helps more people stay engaged.

Why This Matters for What's Next

Nonverbal and paraverbal cues don't create communication styles, but they often reveal them. Over time, patterns emerge, not to label people, but to better understand how they process information and engage with others.

As you become more aware of these signals, you'll start adapting more intentionally.

Next, we'll look at common communication styles and how recognizing preferences can help reduce friction, build trust, and communicate more effectively.

CHAPTER 11. UNDERSTAND FOUR COMMUNICATION STYLES

Research reveals four primary communication styles. Think of them as a spectrum rather than neat little boxes. If aggressive is on one end and passive on the other, assertive would be in the middle. Passive-aggressive combines aspects of both ends of the spectrum.

We may behave differently at work and at home, but we all have a naturally predominant style. To be effective communicators, we need to be aware of our style and adaptable to varying circumstances and people.

> *In the U.S., assertive communication is usually considered the most effective at work.*

What is an Aggressive Communication Style?

An aggressive communicator's message conveys, "I don't care what you want, I don't care what you think. What I say is what matters, and if you believe differently, you're stupid." Their words may or may not be so direct, but aggressors can be. The aggressor wants to win more than solve the problem. An aggressive person tends to take up more space with their body and use more volume with their voice.

An aggressive person controls others through fear. They dominate conversations and activities. An aggressor acts out of anger. They lack concern for others, even violating their rights.

Consequences of the Aggressive Style

Aggressors are often insecure and suffer from low self-esteem. Especially in men, covert depression may manifest as aggression. Aggressors may be impatient, irritable, and angry. They are more likely to suffer from coronary heart disease. Aggressive communicators have fewer close friendships and a higher incidence of divorce.[1]

What is a Passive Communication Style?

At the other end of the spectrum, a passive communicator may not say these words, but the underlying message is, "My feelings don't matter; only yours do. My thoughts aren't important; yours are. I'm nothing. You are superior." A passive individual takes up less space with their body. Their head may be bowed. They might have their arms crossed and their feet close together.

Passive people tend to avoid conflict, go along with the crowd, and give in to unreasonable demands. They hold back opinions, don't give negative feedback, worry about disapproval, and are more apologetic. Passive individuals may be self-effacing at work. They might preface a suggestion with, "This is probably a dumb idea, but..."

Consequences of the Passive Style

People who are passive communicators are more likely to be victims of abuse. Aggressive people seek out passive individuals because they know passive people will do whatever the aggressor wants. Passive individuals fail to have their needs met. They may be resentful and have low self-esteem. Passive communicators may struggle to express thoughts and feelings. This creates frustration for others.

What is an Assertive Communication Style?

Assertive communication balances the needs and rights of both parties. They may not speak these words, but the message of an assertive person is, "Your rights count and so do mine."

> *Assertive communication sounds like:*
> *"This is what I think. This is what I want.*
> *This is how I feel. This is how I see the*
> *situation."*

Assertive communication balances power and looks for a win-win. Assertive body language is confident, not intimidating. Assertive people tend to stand or sit with an open posture and a straight spine. Their voice is controlled emotionally, and their volume is appropriate for the situation.

Assertive people are more direct and honest, able to give opinions, set limits, and stand up for their rights. Assertive people can ask for what they need or want.

Outcomes of Assertive Communication

Assertive communication aligns the needs and rights of both parties. Trust is built with coworkers, family, and friends. Conflict is controlled and often prevented. Important needs are met. Assertive people are often happier and healthier.

What is a Passive-Aggressive Communication Style?

Passive-aggression, sometimes referred to as sugarcoated hostility, is identified by behavior rather than words. A passive-aggressive person appears compliant on the surface but sabotages behind your back. They don't dare to address the real issue (passive), but they want to win, so they "punish" the other party (aggressive).

Passive aggression looks like accidents, forgetting, and backstabbing. A passive-aggressive person might think, "I'll show them! They can't treat me like that! You know what I'm going to do? I'll turn in their paperwork five minutes before the bell rings. We'll see how they like that!"

This kind of behavior exacerbates the wound in the relationship, fails to address the real problem, and results in a hostile, unproductive workplace.

How Assertive Are You?

Here are a few questions that can help you see where you fall on the passive-aggressive spectrum:

- How readily do you ask for your needs to be met?
- Do you say no without excessive guilt?
- How readily do you express your feelings? Can you defend your own beliefs?
- Do you listen to the opinions of others without judging them?
- Can you speak up in a group?
- Do you value your own wisdom?

Also, consider how you are *perceived*. Do others find you passive, assertive, or aggressive?

I had a gentleman take my Assertive Communication class because he worried that his large physical size led others to perceive him as more aggressive than he intended to be. This gentleman learned to take up less space and soften his voice.

If you are very petite, you may wish to adjust your body language and tone of voice to appear more assertive. A woman of small stature may choose to wear high heels at work and exaggerate her posture to appear more assertive.

A Warning About Polarization

When an aggressor and a passive communicator are together, they tend to push each other toward the extremes of the communication style spectrum. Because the aggressor wants to win at all costs and the passive person wants to please others at all costs, they feed each other.

> *It takes an assertive person to subtly guide others toward healthier communication in the middle of the spectrum.*

They do this by modeling the right communication style rather than forcing others to change.

Barriers to Assertive Communication

Three primary barriers to assertive communication are stress, social, and belief barriers.

1. **Stress** or the perception of a threat may trigger our freeze, fight, or flight response.
2. **Social barriers**: our history and habits, or our family and culture, may impact how assertively we communicate.

3. **Belief barriers**: what you believe about yourself, other people, and the way the world works, may hinder your ability to be assertive.

Some cultures don't value assertiveness as highly as others. Be sure to consider cultural expectations in your workplace.

How to Establish an Assertive Style

If you'd like to be more balanced on the communication spectrum, keep reading to learn when to say no, how to be bold at networking events, and remember that you decide what you will and will not do. You have your opinions, and so do others.

> You ARE NOT responsible for other people's problems. Others are not responsible for solving your problems.

If You Tend to Be Perceived as Aggressive and Want to Be Assertive

- Eliminate definitives from your vocabulary, for example, "always" and "never."
- Watch for "you" statements.
- Don't accuse or blame.
- Don't speak as though all other opinions are stupid.
- Cut out extreme words, such as "worst" and "disaster."
- Don't be overly opinionated.
- Consider a more consultative approach to problem-solving at work.
- Allow for others' opinions.
- Don't intimidate, make a personal attack, or use guilt. (Guilt is a poor motivator.)

If You Tend to Be Perceived as Passive and Want to Be Assertive

- Watch for occasions in which you apologize for your opinion, ask permission to participate, downplay your ideas, overjustify, or attack yourself.
- Ask a trusted colleague to help you identify patterns of passive behavior at work.
- When you give opinions, prepare and plan what you will say.
- Breathe, assume a confident posture, and avoid weak opening lines.
- State what you think, want, and need without apology.

Tips for Communicating with a Passive Person

If you're in a leadership position with a passive employee or have a comfortable personal relationship with them, try discussing projects with them *before* a meeting to gauge their opinion. Give them plenty of time to open up. Help them craft an assertive way to present their suggestions.

Your own assertiveness may help draw someone into a more central place on the communication spectrum. Make it clear that their contributions are valued, even if you disagree with them. Nodding, smiling, and making appropriate eye contact may encourage a passive person to continue speaking.

Understanding communication styles helps you adjust how you deliver a message. Being concise determines whether the message lands. When you can say what matters without excess, you reduce friction, save time, and build trust.

CHAPTER 12. BE CONCISE

Spoken language that has multiple superfluous and unnecessary words may sometimes make it difficult for your listeners to not lose interest. You need to keep it simple and easy and concise for them. This is crucially important to always remember.

(Yes, that was intentional.)

Being concise is not about being cold or abrupt. It's about respecting your audience's attention and making it easier for them to understand, remember, and act on what you're saying.

According to William Strunk Jr.'s The Elements of Style:

> "Vigorous writing is concise. A sentence should contain no unnecessary words, a paragraph no unnecessary sentences, for the same reason that a drawing should have no unnecessary lines and a machine no unnecessary parts."[2]

When communication includes too much detail, your audience's attention drifts. Often, people stop listening before we realize they're already convinced. Continuing past that point can dilute your message.

Common tendencies make concision difficult:

- **Fear** often shows up as overexplaining. We talk more because we're worried we haven't said enough.
- **Overconfidence** can lead to rambling because we assume we can "wing it."
- **Time insensitivity** shows up when we forget that our audience has other priorities, pressures, and constraints.

Six Steps to a Concise Message

1. Outline. Whether mental or written, even a brief pause to organize your thoughts improves clarity. Interestingly, the shorter the message, the more preparation it often requires.

Blaise Pascal said:

"I have made this letter longer than usual because I lack the time to make it shorter."[3]

2. Answer the 5 Ws (who, what, where, when, why). These help you stay grounded and avoid unnecessary detours.

3. Tell a story.

4. Observe your audience. Watch for cues: engagement, confusion, restlessness. Adjust as needed.

5. Use images. Images shorten your message, aid memory, and hold attention longer.

6. Listen.

Don't Be TOO Blunt

Concise does not mean curt. Straightforward communication can feel dismissive to relationship-oriented people. Effective communicators adjust based on who they're speaking with and what the situation calls for. The most effective leaders balance clarity with warmth.

Cultural Considerations

Where I live in Wisconsin, people generally expect you to get to the point, whether face-to-face, on the phone, or in a meeting.

Other cultures value more context and relationship-building before business is addressed. As with everything in communication, knowing your audience matters.

Take a Knife to Your Work

In an age of instant access, clarity is a competitive advantage. **Ask yourself: What does my audience need from this? Then remove what doesn't serve that purpose.** That doesn't mean stripping away personality. It means choosing words intentionally.

- Cut jargon.
- Trim unnecessary adjectives.
- Break long sentences in two.
- Use headings and white space to make writing easier to scan.

When you're finished, check whether you actually answered the original question or addressed the core theme.

An important part of everyday communication is knowing how to give and receive feedback. We'll turn to that next.

CHAPTER 13. GIVE EFFECTIVE FEEDBACK

Have you ever worked for someone who only gave feedback once a year during your annual review? By then, the moment has usually passed, habits are entrenched, and the feedback feels more historical than helpful.

Feedback is one of the most effective tools for change when it's timely, specific, and well-intentioned. Feedback works best when it happens early, before a behavior becomes a pattern or erodes trust.

Managers and supervisors are expected to develop people, but effective feedback isn't limited to job titles. Anyone can give feedback that reinforces positive behavior or redirects performance.

Should I Say Something?

Not every irritation needs to become a conversation. The question isn't whether something bothers you; it's whether addressing it serves a purpose. The best advice I've heard was:

> *"If you cannot ignore, forgive, and forget, you need to go and talk to the person. If you cannot go and talk to the*

person, you need to ignore, forgive, and forget."

Before deciding to speak up, ask yourself:

- Is this behavior costing time, money, or momentum?
- Is it affecting customer perception, team morale, or trust?

Addressing issues early keeps them smaller, more objective, and easier to resolve. If the answer is yes, it's worth addressing. If not, you may decide to let it go.

Is It Constructive?

Effective feedback has a purpose. It should clarify expectations, support improvement, or reinforce the behavior you want repeated. If you can't identify a constructive outcome, pause before proceeding.

Both positive and corrective feedback matter. If you only offer praise, it loses meaning. If you only correct, people disengage. Keep feedback focused; one or two points at a time is usually all someone can absorb and act on.

What Happens If I Don't Address It?

Avoiding a conversation doesn't usually resolve the issue; it just delays it. When concerns go unspoken, frustration tends to surface in other ways: tone, body language, or emotional distance.

It's easy to downplay behavior when confrontation feels uncomfortable. We tell ourselves it's not that serious, that it's not our place, or that the timing isn't right. Difficulty alone isn't a reason to avoid feedback.

Ignored long enough, minor issues can turn into bigger ones. That escalation doesn't benefit anyone. Feedback is often the last low-stakes opportunity to course-correct before a situation requires confrontation.

What to Say

Start with the behavior you want to address. Describe what you observed without judgment, labels, or assumptions about intent. Stick to what can be seen or heard.

Say This	Not This
Twice this week, you came in late.	You're lazy and don't care about your job.
When that customer asked for a rollaway bed, you rolled your eyes.	You don't care about our guests.

If It Happens Again

The first conversation is about the behavior. If the same behavior happens again, the conversation shifts to addressing a pattern and whether expectations were met.

If the behavior continues, the issue becomes about the relationship. Trust is affected. At that point, it's reasonable to ask what you want the working relationship to look like going forward.

If you find yourself revisiting the same issue repeatedly, feedback may no longer be enough. That's often a signal that a different kind of conversation is needed. Chapter 42 will get into confrontational discussions.

Feedback Tips

- State the purpose of the conversation and why it matters.
- Describe observable behavior: when, where, who was involved, and the outcome.
- Speak for yourself, avoid "everyone thinks" statements.
- Skip definitives like "always" and "never."
- Give the other person space to respond.
- Listen without interrupting.
- Use open-ended questions to clarify understanding.
- Think of feedback as a dialogue, not a delivery.

End Positively

Suggestions for change should be realistic and specific. Address issues soon after they occur, then show that you're ready to move forward. Offer support. Express confidence in their ability to improve. Summarize what you've agreed on so expectations are clear.

Strong communicators don't just give feedback well; they receive it well, too. That's where we'll go next.

CHAPTER 14. TAKE FEEDBACK AND CRITICISM

When we receive feedback, many of us feel an immediate internal reaction. We may tense up, feel defensive, get emotional, rationalize, or want to explain ourselves. These reactions are human. They don't mean you're bad at communication; they mean something important is being discussed. What matters most is not your first reaction, but what you choose to do next.

Feedback, though often uncomfortable, is one of the most efficient ways to uncover blind spots. When we're willing to treat it as information rather than judgment, it becomes a powerful tool for growth.

One of my closest friends, Gina, was an excellent source of honest feedback. We worked together, carpooled, lived in the same duplex, exercised at the same gym, and volunteered together. Spending that much time with someone makes patterns visible.

From Gina, I learned that not everyone enjoys loud music at 6:00 a.m. on the way to work. I also learned that my well-meaning reassurance, "Everything's going to be fine, "didn't feel reassuring to her when she was facing something serious, like a sibling's cancer diagnosis. My intent was comfort; the impact felt minimizing. That awareness didn't make me a worse friend. It made me more effective.

Pause Before You Respond

Feedback can feel personal because it often touches identity, competence, or belonging. Before responding, give yourself a moment to pause, not to suppress emotion, but to create space.

Your goal isn't to appear unfazed. It's to keep the conversation open.

Overreacting, through defensiveness, dismissal, or visible frustration, can shut down future honesty. A pause helps you stay engaged long enough to hear what's actually being said.

It also helps to remember: not all feedback is delivered skillfully. Giving feedback is difficult, and nervousness may affect how it comes across. Try not to let imperfect delivery distract you from potentially valuable content.

Listen for the Message

You already know how to listen. This is listening under pressure. Avoid interrupting. Ask clarifying questions if something is unclear. Focus on understanding the concern rather than preparing your response. The goal is accuracy, not agreement.

Say Thank You

Acknowledging feedback keeps communication channels open. **Saying thank you doesn't mean you agree; it means you recognize the effort it took to speak up.**

Thank them for sharing their perspective, for their time, and for caring enough about the work or relationship to address it.

Find Out More

Check in with yourself emotionally. If you're feeling overwhelmed or reactive, it's reasonable to ask for time to think. You might say, "I want to reflect on this and respond thoughtfully. Can we revisit this tomorrow?"

If you're calm enough to continue, ask questions to get to the root of the issue:

- What behavior did you observe?
- What impact did it have?
- What would you like to see change?

Avoid asking "why" in a way that sounds like justification or defense. Instead, focus on understanding expectations and outcomes.

Problem-Solving

Feedback often reveals a gap between how we see ourselves and how others experience us. Clarifying that gap is where progress happens. As in the previous section, determine whether the concern is about:

- A specific behavior
- A pattern over time
- The relationship or level of trust

Ask whether the situation was isolated or recurring. Invite suggestions. Treat feedback as data to work with, not a verdict to accept or reject wholesale.

Follow Up

Once you've identified the issue and discussed solutions, thank the person again. Reaffirm your commitment to improvement and set a follow-up point.

Saying something like, "I want to make sure I'm addressing this effectively. Can we check in again in a month?" This reinforces accountability and shows respect for their input.

Poor Timing

Sometimes feedback is delivered at the wrong time or in the wrong setting. If feedback is given publicly, it's often best to acknowledge it briefly and address the concern privately later.

If the Feedback Feels Off-Base

Not all feedback is accurate, but most contains something worth examining. Look for a kernel of truth. Take a step back. Ask yourself whether distance or perspective changes how you view it.

Writing the feedback down and saying it aloud, in your own voice, can help separate the content of the feedback from its delivery. Asking a trusted colleague whether they see the same pattern can add clarity.

If the feedback came from a manager who hasn't gathered input from others affected by your work, it may be appropriate to suggest broader input.

And sometimes, despite your best efforts, the feedback truly doesn't fit. Not everyone will understand you or like your style. Some people are critical by nature. When you've evaluated the feedback honestly and found no useful insight, it's okay to move on.

Receiving feedback well builds credibility. Giving it thoughtfully builds trust. Next, we'll turn to one of the most overlooked ways to strengthen professional relationships: giving meaningful compliments.

CHAPTER 15. GIVE PROFESSIONAL COMPLIMENTS

Positive feedback reinforces the behaviors you want repeated. It balances corrective feedback, builds confidence, and helps people see how their efforts contribute to meaningful outcomes.

A compliment is a small investment with compounding returns. Given consistently, it trains you to notice what's going right, and leaders who look for the good tend to see more of it. But first, let me address one concern that comes up when I speak about compliments.

Have We Overpraised?

In professional settings, the concern usually isn't too much praise, it's credibility. People disengage when recognition feels vague, inflated, or disconnected from real contributions.

Many leaders notice problems quickly but overlook steady, effective work. Being intentional about recognition helps correct that imbalance.

Six Ss of a Professional Compliment

1. Sherlock. Notice first. Effective compliments start with observation. Pay attention to behaviors, habits, and decisions.

2. Small. You don't need a grand achievement. Reliability, preparation, follow-through, and professionalism matter. Look for actions that align with your organization's values and goals.

3. Sincere. Compliments lose power when they're transactional. Speak honestly about what you appreciated and why it mattered.

> Example: "Your attention to detail made the handoff seamless. It saved me time and reduced errors. Thank you!"

4. Specific. Specific praise builds credibility. Avoid generalities that feel inflated or hollow. Focus on a concrete action, skill, or result.

> Example: "Thank you for treating our elderly patients with dignity and respect. That care makes a real difference in their experience."

5. Situational. Choose the setting intentionally. Some people appreciate public recognition; others prefer private acknowledgment. Consider the person, the context, and the impact you want the compliment to have.

6. Swift. Timing matters. Recognition is most meaningful when it's close to the behavior you're reinforcing. Even if you wait to deliver it privately or in writing, don't let too much time pass.

Compliment Others, Grow Yourself

Recognizing excellence sharpens your own awareness. When you can articulate what you value in others, you gain clarity about what matters to you and what you want to model.

A strong compliment can also open the door to learning. Follow recognition with curiosity:

- "You build rapport with new clients so quickly. What helps you find common ground?"
- "You kept the team focused without being heavy-handed. How do you approach that?"

Secondhand compliments are another powerful tool. Sharing positive feedback you've heard about someone reinforces trust without putting anyone on the spot.

> Example: 'I wanted you to know that several attendees mentioned how practical your breakout session was. It clearly resonated."

Traps to Avoid

Be mindful of backhanded compliments, remarks that sound positive but undermine credibility:

- "You're too smart for your own good."
- "I'm impressed you've held a job this long."
- "You look great for your age."

Also, avoid diluting a compliment with qualifiers. Adding "but" or unnecessary commentary weakens the message and shifts focus away from the recognition.

Start Where You Are

You don't need to overhaul your communication style if you don't regularly give compliments. Start by noticing one thing done well today. When recognition becomes part of how you work, compliments feel less like an obligation and more like a natural extension of good communication.

And when compliments come your way, how you receive them matters just as much. Let's look at how to accept them with professionalism and grace.

CHAPTER 16. ACCEPT COMPLIMENTS

Many of us have a reflexive reaction to compliments. We deflect, downplay, joke, self-criticize, narrow the scope, or return the compliment immediately. These responses are common. What matters isn't that the reaction exists, but what it communicates.

When someone offers a compliment, and we dismiss it, we may unintentionally signal discomfort, disbelief, or mistrust of their judgment. That shift transfers the awkwardness back to the giver and can quietly shut down future openness.

- They say, "You did a great job," and we reply, "It was nothing."
- They say, "You look fantastic," and we say, "I got it on sale."

Our intent may be humility. The impact, however, is often confusion.

As with many communication practices, cultural expectations matter. In some cultures, downplaying compliments is a sign of respect. Context always applies.

Why Compliments Feel Hard to Take

People deny or deflect compliments for a variety of reasons, most of them rooted in self-protection rather than ego.

- Concern about appearing conceited. We worry that accepting praise sounds like agreeing with it.
- Low confidence or self-doubt. Positive feedback doesn't align with how we see ourselves.
- Discounting our own effort. We assume others didn't see the missteps, shortcuts, or help we received.
- Discomfort with attention. We shift the spotlight quickly to restore balance.
- Suspicion. We question motives and assume praise comes with strings attached.

Awareness of these tendencies is enough. You don't need to fix them, just recognize when they're driving your response.

What Acceptance Signals

Accepting a compliment isn't about ego. It's about professionalism. A simple "thank you" acknowledges the giver's perspective without endorsing or inflating it. It keeps communication open and signals that positive or constructive feedback is welcome.

When compliments are consistently denied or deflected, people are less likely to offer them again. Over time, that can reduce not only recognition but also honest feedback more broadly.

If a leader or colleague senses that you struggle to receive praise, they may hesitate to offer constructive input. Accepting compliments well helps establish you as someone who can handle feedback of all kinds.

Tips for Professional Acceptance

- **Assume good intent.** Most compliments are sincere.
- **Receive before responding**. You don't need to explain, justify, or qualify.

- **Separate humility from denial**. Gratitude doesn't require self-deprecation.
- **Let it land**. Sometimes the most respectful response is simply to allow the compliment to stand.

A self-aware communicator knows their strengths as well as their growth areas. If maintaining humility is important to you, a stand-alone "thank you" is often enough.

If you're ready, you might add:

- "I appreciate you noticing."
- "That means a lot."
- "I worked hard on that."

There may be rare moments when the giver's enthusiasm feels excessive or performative. In those cases, a brief, neutral acknowledgment shows appreciation without feeding egos.

A Skill Worth Practicing

Accepting compliments is deceptively simple and surprisingly difficult. Like any communication skill, it improves with intention and repetition.

It also sets the stage for the next challenge: knowing when and how to decline requests, invitations, or expectations without damaging relationships. Next, we'll look at how to say no with clarity, confidence, and respect.

CHAPTER 17. KNOW WHEN AND HOW TO SAY NO

No is a complete sentence. It's also a strategic one.

Saying no isn't about being difficult or unhelpful. It's about making intentional choices with your time, energy, and attention. Every yes commits you to something and quietly takes those resources away from something else.

Why Saying No Feels So Hard

For many people, the barrier isn't logical; it's fear. Fear of judgment. Fear of disappointing someone. Fear of losing status, opportunity, or connection.

So we say yes when we shouldn't. And while the yes may sound agreeable in the moment, the cost shows up later as resentment, exhaustion, or disengagement. Over time, that erodes trust. Clear communication isn't about pleasing everyone. It's about being honest about what you can and cannot sustain.

When to Say No

A no may be the right choice when a request:

- Competes with existing priorities or commitments
- Consumes more time or energy than you realistically have

- Interferes with your core responsibilities
- Creates financial, reputational, or personal strain
- Pushes you out of alignment with your values

Saying no often protects something important that's already on your plate.

Saying No to Too Much Work

Too much work can look like success until it isn't. There was a stretch when I said yes to too many projects in a row. The extra income didn't offset the missed evenings, the distraction, or the ripple effects at home. The signal I was sending to clients was that my availability was unlimited. It wasn't.

One practical way to signal capacity is through boundaries: timelines, scope, or price. My dad once told me that if I was landing every job and constantly overwhelmed, I was probably underpricing my work.

That principle applies whether you're self-employed or salaried. Your calendar, responsiveness, and commitments all communicate what you're willing to carry.

How to Say No

You don't need a script, but here's what I've found that helps.

- **Buy yourself time.** "Let me take a look at my schedule and get back to you."
- **Wait to be asked.** Volunteering prematurely often turns into an obligation.
- **State the no clearly and respectfully.** "I won't be able to take this on, but I appreciate you thinking of me."
- **Offer an alternative when appropriate.** "I'm not available, but Susan may be; would you like an introduction?"

- **Align your words and body language.** Mixed signals invite pushback.

Excessive apologies or long explanations often dilute the message. A brief reason is fine; a list of justifications usually isn't necessary.

A no may close one door, and that's okay. It often keeps several others open.

Letting go of Guilt

Guilt thrives when decisions are made on the spot.

One thing that's helped me is deciding in advance where my time and energy will go. Each year, I choose which organizations I volunteer with and how much unpaid work I'll take on. When a request doesn't fit, I can respond with an honest no.

Language matters here. "Should" tends to carry guilt. Reframing choices around capacity and intention makes decisions clearer and easier to stand behind.

Moving Forward

Saying no well reinforces trust. People may not love the answer, but they'll respect the clarity.

As communication moves increasingly into digital spaces where tone, body language, and timing are harder to read, being intentional about boundaries becomes even more important. Next, we'll look at how communication changes when the medium does.

SECTION 4: DIGITAL COMMUNICATION

CHAPTER 18. KEEP UP WITH TECHNOLOGY

As a marketing consultant, I often review websites. Occasionally, I'll find something that immediately raises a red flag, not because it's "old," but because it signals inattention. I recently reviewed a website for a finance company. The website had a picture of a flip phone on its homepage. Yes, a flip phone.

When technology looks neglected, people wonder what else is being overlooked. Technology communicates. Whether we intend it or not, our tools send a message about relevance, credibility, and care.

How Our World Changes

The shelf life of our technology is about as long as a tuna fish sandwich. Technology evolves quickly. Tools change. Platforms rise and fall. What matters isn't mastering everything; it's staying adaptable.

Entire industries have been reshaped by new ways of connecting, buying, sharing, and collaborating. The common thread isn't a specific app or device; it's communication that's accessible, responsive, and reasonably current. You don't always need the newest thing. You do need to avoid getting stuck.

Why This Matters for Communication

Effective communicators understand that technology is an amplifier. Used well, it removes friction. Used poorly or ignored, it creates doubt. Staying current helps you:

- Communicate efficiently across teams and locations
- Maintain credibility with clients, colleagues, and partners
- Share information clearly and consistently
- Reduce unnecessary back-and-forth and confusion

This isn't about being tech-savvy for status. It's about choosing tools that support clarity, continuity, and connection.

Principles That Age Well

Instead of chasing trends, focus on these enduring questions:

- **Does this tool make communication easier or harder?**
- **Does it help people access what they need, when they need it?**
- **Is it widely understood by the people we serve?**
- **Does it support how we actually work, not how we wish we worked?**

Technology should serve the message, not overshadow it.

Stay Aware (Without Being Overwhelmed)

You don't need to monitor everything. Choose a few reliable sources that help you see what's changing and why it matters. Look outside your industry occasionally. Some of the best ideas come from spaces that solve similar problems in different ways.

Learn What's Worth Learning

When new tools are introduced at work, approach them with curiosity. Understanding the basics often puts you ahead of those who avoid learning altogether.

Professional development, experimentation, and asking questions all signal adaptability, an increasingly valuable communication trait.

Moving Forward

Technology will continue to change. Communication fundamentals won't. Next, we'll look at one of the most visible and misunderstood tools in modern communication: social media, and how you might choose to use it thoughtfully at work.

CHAPTER 19. USE SOCIAL MEDIA LIKE A PRO

Before you post anything, ask one question: What is my objective?

Are you using social platforms to stay personally connected, support your career, or both? Different goals require different choices. Social media is a tool. Like any tool, its value depends on how and why you use it.

The Tradeoffs

Social media can be a time drain. It can also blur boundaries. Even with privacy settings in place, content can be reshared or misunderstood. A good rule that doesn't age: **If you wouldn't want it quoted publicly, don't post it.**

Why It's Worth Using (When Used Well)

Social platforms allow people to get to know who they're working with, hiring, or buying from. That builds trust.

Most decisions, professional and personal, have an emotional component. Seeing the humans behind a brand or title reduces friction and builds rapport. When used intentionally, social media supports credibility and connection.

Learn the Room Before You Speak

A common professional misstep is treating every platform the same. Think of each network like a different gathering. You wouldn't walk into a room and immediately dominate the conversation or pitch yourself. First, observe. Pay attention to:

- Tone and pacing
- What people share (and what they don't)
- What gets engagement
- Who the audience really is

Then decide how and whether you want to participate.

Common Missteps to Avoid

- Posting controversial or inflammatory content that distracts from your professional goals
- Oversharing personal details that don't serve your audience
- Posting so frequently that people wonder if you ever log off
- Sharing content without checking accuracy or context

If a post doesn't inform, help, or connect, it may not need to be shared.

Professional Best Practices

- Know your organization's guidelines and expectations
- Never share confidential or sensitive information
- Proofread and fact-check before posting
- Be cautious with humor; tone doesn't always translate
- Protect access: use strong passwords, multiple admins, and good account hygiene
- If you make a mistake, acknowledge it promptly and professionally

Use Social Media to Support Your Career

Social media is only one part of a well-rounded professional presence. The goal isn't visibility for its own sake; it's alignment. Quality matters more than quantity. Thoughtful connections outperform large, disengaged audiences. Use social platforms to:

- Share insights your audience finds useful
- Highlight work you're proud of (without overselling)
- Learn from others in and outside your industry
- Stay visible without being noisy

Consistency helps. So does clarity. Your profile, tone, and content should reinforce the same professional story.

Measurement, Not Obsession

Pay attention to what resonates. You don't need to track everything, but noticing patterns helps you adjust to your audience's expectations. Ask:

- What type of content sparks conversation?
- What falls flat?
- What aligns best with my goals?

Things That Rarely End Well Online

Some advice never expires:

- Don't post when impaired or overly emotional
- Don't engage in online arguments
- Don't ask questions you could easily research
- Don't post low-quality visuals on visual platforms
- Don't change your professional identity constantly
- When in doubt, pause.

Moving Forward

Used thoughtfully, social media reinforces trust. Used carelessly, it erodes it.

As communication becomes increasingly global, understanding how messages land across cultures matters more than ever. Next, we'll explore how to communicate sensitively and effectively across cultural differences.

SECTION 5: COMMUNICATE ACROSS CULTURES

CHAPTER 20. COMMUNICATE ACROSS CULTURES

Culture refers to the groups and communities shaped by shared experiences. Culture influences how we see the world, interpret meaning, and communicate. Most of us belong to many cultures at once.

Some cultures we're born into, such as nationality, language, or class. Others we acquire over time through education, career paths, geography, changes in economic status, or life-altering events. Culture is not static. Neither are we.

Understanding this matters because communication doesn't happen in a vacuum. It happens between people with different assumptions, histories, and norms.

Cross-Cultural Communication

Modern work allows us to collaborate across borders, time zones, and lived experiences. You can work with someone across the globe as readily as someone down the hall. This access is powerful, and it raises the stakes. When communication breaks down, it's not always about skill or intent. Often, it's about context.

Start with Awareness

Awareness begins with acknowledging that we all bring bias into communication. Bias isn't a moral failure; it's human. What matters is whether we notice it and stay open to learning. Consider taking the Implicit Association Test by Harvard. You can find it at https://implicit.harvard.edu/.

Our own culture shapes how we interpret tone, silence, directness, humor, and authority. What feels clear or efficient to one person may feel abrupt or dismissive to another.

Even shared language doesn't guarantee shared meaning. American, British, and Australian English differ more than we realize. Awareness helps prevent overconfidence.

Benefit from Diverse Perspectives

Organizations benefit from diverse perspectives because better decisions come from broader input. When teams include varied experiences, blind spots shrink.

At the same time, people from historically marginalized or underrepresented groups may hesitate to speak up, especially in large settings. Creating space for contribution often requires intentional design, not louder voices. Small-group discussions, structured turn-taking, or inviting written input can help surface ideas that might otherwise go unheard.

Build Relationships First

Cross-cultural communication improves when relationships come first. Trust takes time, especially when someone has experienced exclusion or misunderstanding.

Be proactive, respectful, and patient. Learn when you can. Ask questions when appropriate. Avoid assuming that your way or the majority's way is the default. If you misspeak or misunderstand, treat it as information, not failure. A sincere apology and willingness to learn go a long way.

Support Your Team

Clear communication becomes even more important across multicultural teams. Simple language, fewer idioms, and thoughtful pacing reduce confusion. Humor can build rapport, but it's also highly culture-specific, so use it carefully.

Modeling curiosity, respect, and adaptability sets the tone for others to do the same. One-on-one conversations often create more psychological safety than group settings. Consider practical realities, too: time zones, holidays, and individual communication preferences.

This chapter is only an introduction to cross-cultural communication. The real work happens in practice, through listening, observing, and staying open.

Next, we'll explore another dimension of difference that shows up daily at work: communicating across generations.

SECTION 6: COMMUNICATE WITH ANY GENERATION

CHAPTER 21. OVERCOME GENERATIONAL MYOPIA

You've heard it. Perhaps you've even said it yourself:

"Young people today have NO work ethic!"

This reaction is understandable. Work has changed. Expectations have shifted. What feels normal to one generation can feel foreign or frustrating to another. The trouble begins when we treat those differences as flaws rather than as context.

A single sentence like that doesn't just describe behavior; it assigns motive, values, and character to an entire group of people. That's a heavy lift for any generalization.

Look Back

Every generation has been misunderstood before it was understood. The Greatest Generation was once called the Lost Generation. Boomers were labeled spoiled and reluctant to grow up. Gen Xers were dismissed as cynical complainers. Millennials have been described as entitled and narcissistic.

Time has a way of reframing these narratives. What looks like irresponsibility in the moment often turns out to be adaptation.

Much of what we interpret as a "generational trait" is really a mix of life stage, lived experience, and the environment people grew up navigating. As newer generations enter the workforce, we have a choice: repeat the pattern or interrupt it.

What Is Myopia?

Myopia is a vision condition where what's close is clear, but what's farther away is blurry. Figuratively, myopia shows up when we rely too heavily on our own perspective and assume it's universal. We see what feels familiar clearly and misinterpret what doesn't.

Erin Meyer, in *The Culture Map*, explains that when we assume differences don't matter, we default to judging others through our own lens.[4]

The same is true generationally. When we dismiss generational context, we're more likely to misunderstand behavior and assign intent that isn't there. Generational myopia isn't about bad intentions. It's about a limited perspective.

The Cure for Generational Myopia

The goal isn't to stereotype people based on their birth year. It's to recognize that shared experiences shape expectations, communication norms, and work habits.

If you catch yourself thinking, "They just don't want to work," pause and ask instead: *How might work look different to someone who grew up in a different environment than I did?*

Digital natives, for example, may never feel "off the clock" in the same way previous generations did. That doesn't mean they care less; it often means they work differently.

Language matters here. Broad phrases like "always," "never," or "that's just how they are" shut down curiosity and reinforce distance. Replacing judgment with questions keeps communication open and productive.

Believing the best in people doesn't mean ignoring performance issues. It means addressing them accurately rather than making assumptions.

Why This Matters

Understanding generational context helps us communicate more clearly, lead more effectively, and avoid unnecessary friction. These frameworks aren't rules; they're reference points. They help us anticipate differences, not assign limitations.

In the chapters that follow, we'll look at how different generations tend to approach work and communication, broadening your lens and improving how you connect, collaborate, and lead.

CHAPTER 22. WORK WELL WITH TRADITIONALS

Traditionals, sometimes called the Silent Generation or the Greatest Generation, were born in 1945 or earlier. Many came of age during the Great Depression and were shaped by scarcity, uncertainty, and significant global events. Frugality, resilience, and perseverance were often necessary for survival.

While Traditionals represent a small portion of today's workforce, some remain actively engaged as volunteers, board members, mentors, and advisors.

Changes to the Workplace

The workplace has changed dramatically since Traditionals first entered it. Business hours have expanded. Technology has transformed how and where work gets done. More women participate in the workforce, and career paths are less linear.

My maternal grandparents owned a hardware store in Beaver Dam, Wisconsin. They moved there to run the store, which they did successfully for decades. When they decided to sell it, my grandmother wrote in her memoirs:

> "Nothing lasts forever and times they were a changing again. Shopko moved in at the edge of town with a huge parking lot. They were open seven days a week along

with evening hours. Meanwhile downtown we still had parking meters, (only open one night a week), and closed on Sundays. It was happening all over the country."

Her reflection captures something many Traditionals experienced firsthand: rapid change that disrupted long-standing ways of working and doing business.

The Value of Traditionals in the Workplace

According to *Generations, Inc.*, by Meagan Johnson and Larry Johnson, older workers often bring stability and consistency to organizations, including lower absenteeism, lower turnover, strong commitment to quality, and dependability.[5]

Traditionals frequently pass along skills that are less formally taught today: professional etiquette, organizational awareness, and interpersonal communication.

Traditionals as Volunteers

Many Traditionals contribute through volunteering and community involvement. Show respect by using appropriate titles, clearly defining roles, and expressing genuine appreciation.

Communicating with Traditionals

Some Traditionals may prefer familiar processes or established routines, particularly when those systems have worked well for years.

While preferences vary by individual, some Traditionals appreciate tangible acknowledgment such as a plaque, certificate, or written recognition of service. Many value being recognized for reliability, stewardship, and long-term contribution.

Traditionals often want to contribute to a larger purpose. Explaining how their work or volunteer role fits into the broader mission can increase engagement.

Capture and Apply Their Wisdom

Knowledge transfer becomes critical when experienced individuals step away from their roles, whether they are Traditionals, Boomers, or any long-tenured employee. Make sure you capture:

- **Explicit knowledge** includes documented processes and procedures.
- **Implicit knowledge** develops through experience and practice and is harder to articulate.
- **Tacit knowledge** comes from intuition, pattern recognition, and lived experience.

Tacit knowledge is often the hardest to capture because it lives in experience rather than documentation. **It's why, even when you follow the same recipe, Grandma's pie always turns out better than yours.** She doesn't measure precisely. She knows when the dough *feels* right. She adjusts based on humidity, temperature, and instinct built over decades. That kind of knowledge requires patience, observation, and open-ended questions to transfer. Creating space for experienced employees to explain not just what they do, but how they decide, is essential before that wisdom walks out the door.

Set Up Mentor Relationships

More seasoned employees often mentor new ones. Reverse mentoring adds value by allowing knowledge to flow in both directions. Reverse mentoring helps close skill gaps, reduces "us versus them" thinking, and strengthens cross-generational relationships. Younger employees may share insights on emerging tools or trends, while experienced professionals offer a strategic perspective and institutional memory.

For mentoring relationships to work well:

- Identify a specific need or skill gap
- Be clear about expectations and time commitment
- Treat the exchange as mutual learning
- Acknowledge and appreciate contributions on both sides

Next, we'll move along the generational continuum to Baby Boomers, where we'll continue to see how experience, expectations, and communication styles evolve and overlap more than we might expect.

CHAPTER 23. WORK WELL WITH BABY BOOMERS

Baby Boomers were born between 1946 and 1964, following World War II during a period of rapid population growth and economic expansion. Many grew up in crowded schools and competitive environments, which often required collaboration, persistence, and adaptability.

Influential voices during their formative years encouraged boomers to question authority, redefine family roles, and expand opportunities, particularly for women. These forces contributed to a generation that often values purpose, contribution, and progress alongside achievement.

The Value of Boomers in the Workplace

Baby Boomers continue to represent a significant portion of the workforce. Many bring decades of experience across multiple economic cycles, organizational structures, and leadership models.

Many Boomers offer perspective, creativity, and empathy shaped by long careers. Their track records often make them credible leaders, effective mentors, and trusted partners in client-facing roles. Boomers are also well positioned to bridge eras of work, having adapted from more hierarchical, analog workplaces to increasingly collaborative, digital ones.

Communicating with Boomers

Many Boomers developed strong interpersonal communication skills and tend to be comfortable with face-to-face conversations and phone calls. They often appreciate context and clarity and may prefer having sufficient information before making decisions.

Team-based approaches tend to resonate. Clear goals, defined roles, and step-by-step plans can support alignment, particularly on larger projects. That said, communication preferences vary widely, and flexibility remains key.

Effectively Managing Boomers

Avoid assuming that Boomers are eager or expected to exit the workforce. Many continue working by choice, out of interest, or out of necessity. Keeping work engaging and meaningful supports retention and morale.

Mentorship opportunities can be mutually beneficial. Boomers often make strong mentors for Gen X, Millennials, and Gen Z, particularly in leadership, client relations, and institutional knowledge.

Flexibility matters. Some Boomers leave roles due to health considerations or caregiving responsibilities. Offering flexible schedules, part-time options, or supportive benefits can help organizations retain experienced talent.

As we move along the generational continuum, we'll see both contrast and continuity. Next up is Generation X, a group shaped by different forces but often bridges Boomers and younger generations in practical ways.

CHAPTER 24. WORK WELL WITH GEN XERS

Generation Xers were born between 1965 and 1976, during a period of significant social and economic transition. Family structures were changing, dual-income households became more common, and many Gen Xers learned early how to manage independence and responsibility.

Described as "latchkey kids," many Gen Xers came home from school to empty houses and learned to organize their time, complete responsibilities, and solve problems. **This early independence shaped how they approach work.**

Gen X also grew up during economic uncertainty. They watched institutions change, companies downsize, and long-term employment disappear. As a result, **they tend to be pragmatic about work and cautious about promises**. Their loyalty is often directed toward meaningful work, trustworthy leaders, and outcomes, not institutions alone.

They came of age alongside rapid changes in media and technology. This generation is comfortable with speed, efficiency, and self-directed learning. They tend to value productivity and dislike unnecessary friction.

Later in life, many Gen Xers intentionally built the family stability they lacked earlier. As a result, they often require clear reasons to sacrifice personal or family time for work.

The Value of Gen Xers at Work

From an early age, Gen Xers were accustomed to making decisions independently. What is sometimes labeled as cynicism is more accurately described as critical thinking. They question assumptions, spot inefficiencies, and look for practical solutions.

Gen X leaders are often entrepreneurial, adaptable, and resourceful. They **tend to be comfortable working autonomously and leading without micromanagement**. They frequently serve as stabilizers within organizations, bridging experience with innovation.

Gen Xers value development and mentorship, though they may not seek constant social interaction at work. They are often effective coaches.

Communicating with Gen X

Gen Xers tend to appreciate clear, efficient, and respectful communication that respects their time. They value asynchronous communication that allows them to process information and respond thoughtfully. They expect follow-through. If a message is sent, they assume it matters. Clarity, context, and timeliness build trust with this group.

Managing Generation X

One of the most meaningful benefits for Gen Xers is flexibility. Many are balancing work with caregiving responsibilities. Flexibility in schedule, location, and structure often matters more than perks.

Gen Xers frequently ask, "If the work gets done well, why does it matter when or where it happens?" **Organizations that reward results rather than presence tend to earn their loyalty.**

Gen Xers prefer to be asked rather than told. They respond well to autonomy and accountability and expect recognition based on merit rather than tenure. Rules that lack purpose will be questioned.

This generation usually thrives when challenged and given room to work. Provide clear expectations, meaningful feedback, and space to execute. Check in periodically, not to hover, but to ensure alignment and prevent burnout.

Next, we'll look at a microgeneration that sits between Gen X and Millennials, often shaped by both analog and digital worlds, and how that unique positioning influences communication and work styles.

CHAPTER 25. WORK WELL WITH XENNIALS

Xennials don't quite fit with their older siblings, Generation X, and they didn't grow up as full digital natives like Millennials. (I'm a Xennial, but my oldest sister is an X, and my youngest sister is a Millennial. And let me tell you, we are from different generations!)

If you've ever felt comfortable translating between generations or caught yourself thinking, I get *both* sides of this you may be an Xennial too.

Xennials are a microgeneration born between 1977 and 1985. Sometimes called the Oregon Trail Generation, they experienced an analog childhood and a digital adulthood. They grew up during a period of rapid transition, which shaped how they communicate, work, and adapt. That in-between perspective is what makes them especially valuable at work.

What Shapes Xennials?

Technology is the reason this microgeneration exists. Xennials came of age during a seismic shift, from physical to digital, that permanently influenced how they learn, evaluate information, and adopt change.

In school, Xennials used card catalogs and physical books because early websites weren't considered credible sources. They remember writing in cursive, even if they don't send handwritten letters today. They learned research, patience, and verification before "search" became instantaneous.

Many Xennials had home computers by middle school (remember dial-up?), found early chat rooms, and participated in anonymous online forums long before social media was widely used. (Does that guy I met in a chat room count as a first boyfriend?)

Like many Xennials, I'm grateful that social media didn't exist during my most awkward teen years. I made questionable fashion choices and plenty of poor decisions without leaving a digital footprint. I was on Myspace briefly. When I joined Facebook, I needed an invitation.

Xennials are often early adopters of technology, but not unquestioning ones. And they're comfortable stepping away from their devices, taking tech-free vacations, and putting phones down at dinner. Technology is a tool, not an identity.

Many Xennials benefited from relative economic stability early in adulthood, which gave many of them time to explore educational paths, take gap years, or experiment professionally. That freedom helped shape a strong desire for work that aligns with values, not just titles.

The Value of Xennials at Work

Like most cusp generations, Xennials act as conduits. They can communicate comfortably with older and younger colleagues and often serve as informal translators between styles, expectations, and tools.

Xennials grew up using landlines and speaking to friends' parents. They're comfortable with phone calls, face-to-face conversations, and written communication. At the same time, they understand digital collaboration, remote work, and emerging platforms.

This generation didn't grow up constantly connected, but they adapted quickly. **That combination makes most Xennials particularly effective at change management, cross-generational leadership, and bridging communication gaps.**

Communicating with Xennials

Xennials are digital immigrants with analog instincts. They understand both worlds and expect inclusive, respectful communication. They don't want assumptions made about gender roles, family structures, or life choices.

Managing Xennials

Life stage matters more than age for Xennials. Where they are personally and professionally will strongly influence what they value at work.

Many Xennials learned early to diversify through side hustles, freelance work, or multiple skill sets to stay resilient during economic uncertainty. Encourage that entrepreneurial thinking inside your organization rather than viewing it as a distraction.

When it comes to new technology, Xennials tend to evaluate before committing. They read reviews, compare options, and consider long-term implications. **This makes them excellent beta testers, implementation leads, and advisors during transitions.**

Give Xennials autonomy, context, and trust. They don't need micromanagement, but they tend to appreciate clarity, purpose, and feedback. When engaged well, they often become steady leaders who help organizations evolve without losing institutional knowledge.

Next, we'll take a closer look at Millennials and how their fully digital upbringing shapes the modern workplace.

CHAPTER 26. WORK WELL WITH MILLENNIALS

I once gave a presentation on working with Millennials for a tech group. It was an after-hours event, drinks were flowing, and we kicked things off with a live, phone-based quiz. The group did exceptionally well identifying Millennials' strengths: collaboration, adaptability, purpose-driven work, yet laughed through the entire exercise and repeatedly referred to Millennials as lazy and lacking a work ethic.

That disconnect is worth paying attention to. When people can correctly describe a generation's strengths but still dismiss them, the issue is deeply seated. Let's learn a little bit about who Millennials are and how to work best with them.

Millennials Size and Influence

Millennials represent a significant portion of today's workforce and an even larger share of cultural and purchasing influence. More importantly, they don't just participate in systems; they shape them.

Millennials expect organizations to take positions, act ethically, and contribute beyond profit. That expectation shows up in how they choose employers, products, and partners. Whether we agree with those expectations or not, they influence how business gets done.

Why the Misconceptions Persist

Many of the tensions surrounding Millennials stem from differences in their work habits. Their communication is more constant. Their values are expressed more publicly.

To older generations, that can appear unfocused or entitled. To Millennials, it feels efficient and honest. What's often labeled as "lack of work ethic" is usually a mismatch in how effort is displayed.

Shaped by Connection

Millennials grew up during a time of increased parental involvement and rapid technological expansion. As a result, many are accustomed to frequent feedback, access to information, and ongoing dialogue. This doesn't mean they can't work independently. It means they're used to collaboration and transparency being part of the process.

Technically Fluent, Socially Connected

Millennials didn't just adopt technology; they integrated it into how they think, organize, and communicate. **They are comfortable using digital tools to streamline work, share information, and stay connected.** Leaders who leverage that fluency often see gains in efficiency and engagement.

Integrating Work and Life

Millennials tend to blur the lines between professional and personal life. They don't always separate "on" and "off" the way previous generations did. Continuous connection means they may address work issues outside traditional hours and handle personal matters during the workday. From their perspective, it balances out. The key isn't monitoring time. It's clarifying outcomes.

Optimism with Purpose

Despite growing up amid economic uncertainty, global crises, and constant news exposure, Millennials tend to be optimistic about their ability to create change. That optimism fuels their interest in sustainability, equity, and community impact.

If your organization wants to launch an initiative focused on responsibility or long-term impact, Millennials are often eager to lead.

Making the Most of Millennials at Work

Millennials tend to respond well to workplaces that allow them to question outdated rules, invite participation, and explain the "why" behind decisions. They're more engaged when expectations are clear, and their contributions are visible. They benefit from frequent interaction. Transparency matters, especially around what information is shareable and what isn't.

Teams Over Hierarchy

Traditional top-down leadership tends to be less effective with Millennials, who were raised working in teams and collaborative environments. They're more motivated by shared ownership than rigid structure.

As we'll see next, many of these trends don't stop with Millennials. Some intensify. Others shift. Let's take a closer look at what changes as we turn to Generation Z.

CHAPTER 27. WORK WELL WITH GEN Z

Born between 1997 and 2012, Generation Z entered the workforce during a period shaped by economic disruption, rapid technological change, and shifting expectations around work, leadership, and stability. Many grew up watching parents lose jobs during the Great Recession and older Millennial siblings struggle under student debt. These experiences profoundly shaped how Gen Z approaches work, money, and authority.

Generation Z has been online at high speed since early childhood. As true digital natives, they tend to be comfortable navigating information-rich environments and switching between tools quickly. While they rely heavily on technology, many Gen Zers place a high value on face-to-face communication for meaningful conversations, feedback, and trust-building.

Gen Z and Education

Rising tuition costs and the visibility of student debt have pushed many Gen Zers to rethink traditional education. Apprenticeships, certifications, trade programs, and employer-sponsored training are increasingly attractive.

Many organizations are already welcoming Gen Z into full-time roles, internships, and freelance work. Early exposure to real-world work has accelerated Gen Z's expectations for skill development, feedback, and clarity.

The Value of Gen Z at Work

Generation Z is no longer a future workforce; it is a present one. Gen Z makes up a growing share of entry- and mid-level roles across industries, including manufacturing, healthcare, technology, and professional services.

Research consistently shows that Gen Z values honesty, integrity, and financial stability in leadership more than prestige or rapid advancement. A 2023 Deloitte Global Gen Z Survey found these traits ranked higher than titles or status.[6]

Unlike Millennials, who entered the workforce during a period of relative economic optimism, Gen Z came of age amid volatility. As a result, many are pragmatic, risk-aware, and outcome-focused. They value independence. They want flexibility, but also structure. Gen Z brings measurable strengths to the workplace:

- Speed to competence. Raised in information-dense environments, Gen Z adapts quickly to new systems.
- Efficiency and experimentation. Gen Z employees are comfortable testing, iterating, and improving processes, especially digital ones.
- Values alignment. Sustainability, transparency, and ethical practices strongly influence where Gen Z chooses to work and who they trust.
- Comfort with hybrid work. Having normalized digital collaboration early, Gen Z navigates remote and hybrid environments with ease.

At the same time, Gen Z benefits from guidance around prioritization, context, and professional norms, areas where more experienced colleagues add tremendous value. **When organizations intentionally pair Gen Z's technical fluency with seasoned judgment, performance improves.**

Communicating with Gen Z

Despite assumptions to the contrary, many Gen Zers prefer in-person communication for feedback, coaching, and important conversations. Digital tools are efficient, but trust is built face-to-face.

Gen Z is accustomed to fast feedback loops and clear signals of progress. This can look like impatience, but it is often a desire for clarity. Encouraging deeper thinking, asking them to explain their reasoning, and modeling how to present ideas professionally builds long-term capability.

Gen Z also expects transparency. Growing up in an environment where information is widely shared, they want to understand decisions, priorities, and tradeoffs. When they don't, they may fill in gaps on their own.

Managing Generation Z

Be flexible and curious. Managers who approach Gen Z with openness tend to uncover their value more quickly.

Provide structure with autonomy. Routine creates accountability and supports learning, even in flexible environments. Clear expectations, defined roles, and written job descriptions help Gen Z succeed.

Correct early and clearly. Inexperience means just that. Explain what may seem obvious, but avoid talking down. Immediate, respectful feedback prevents minor issues from becoming habits.

Show them how to grow. Gen Z wants to understand what progress looks like. Even a short-term or "micro" career path increases engagement and retention.

Treat them like valued coworkers. Culture fit matters deeply to this generation. Pair new hires with a buddy or mentor who can help them navigate both the work and the unwritten rules.

Recognize merit. For Gen Z, credibility comes from ideas and contributions, not tenure. This trend will continue, and in many organizations, it's already working.

Close the Generation Gap

Embrace collaborative work. Many Gen Zers were raised on team sports and group projects. Create environments where creativity and problem-solving are visible and shared.

Lead by example. Every generation learns from the one before it. How we communicate, give feedback, and show respect sets the tone for what follows.

When I first published this book, my Gen Z son was ten years old. At the time, I could only speculate about how his generation might show up at work. At 13, he started his first business. Now he's seventeen and in good company with other teenagers already working. Gen Z entered the workforce early through part-time jobs, gig work, content creation, and entrepreneurship, and we've learned a lot by watching them work in real time. That shift matters because Gen Alpha is next.

CHAPTER 28. WORK WELL WITH GEN ALPHA

Just this week, I met with two moms of Gen Alpha boys who already have businesses in art, design, and apparel. They weren't asking whether their kids *should* work. They were asking how to set them up for success.

That tells us something important: Gen Alpha won't arrive at work someday. They're already practicing for it.

Who Is Gen Alpha?

Generation Alpha includes those born between 2013 and 2025. They are the first generation fully born into an AI-assisted, algorithm-driven world. Voice interfaces, personalized learning, and on-demand answers are typical for them, not innovations. Like every generation before them, Gen Alpha is being shaped by the conditions of their upbringing:

- Rapid technological acceleration
- Increased entrepreneurship at younger ages
- Parents and educators who witnessed economic disruption firsthand
- A world where learning, creating, and earning often overlap

As with Gen Z, many traits attributed to Gen Alpha are as much about age and life stage as generation. The real opportunity is not labeling them, but preparing leaders.

What's Already Emerging

Early research and observation suggest several trends worth paying attention to, not as predictions, but as signals.

They expect agency early. Gen Alpha is growing up in environments that encourage self-expression, customization, and choice. This doesn't mean they resist structure; it means they are likely to respond better when they understand *why* something matters.

They are creators. Whether through art, design, coding, or digital products, Gen Alpha is accustomed to producing, not just consuming. For leaders, this shifts the question from *"How do I motivate them?"* to *"How do I channel what they're already building?"*

They are AI-native. Gen Alpha will not experience artificial intelligence as a disruption. It will be infrastructure. Leaders will need to focus less on tool adoption and more on **judgment, ethics, and critical thinking**, skills that technology cannot replace.

They learn by doing. Formal education is no longer the sole or even primary source of skill development. Apprenticeships, project-based learning, and real-world experimentation will matter more than credentials alone.

The Value Gen Alpha Will Bring to Work

It's too early to define Gen Alpha by outcomes, but not too early to see potential. Gen Alpha is likely to bring:

- High comfort with complexity
- Strong visual and spatial communication skills
- Entrepreneurial instincts
- A practical understanding of digital systems

- A desire for meaningful contribution, not just participation

As with Gen Z, their effectiveness at work will depend less on their generation and more on how well leaders:

- Set expectations
- Teach professional judgment
- Model communication
- Create psychological safety

Communicating with Gen Alpha

Gen Alpha will not need less communication. They will need **clearer** communication. They are growing up in environments where information is abundant, but context is not always obvious. Leaders who succeed with Gen Alpha will:

- Explain reasoning, not just rules
- Be explicit about expectations
- Invite questions without interpreting them as resistance
- Balance speed with reflection

Face-to-face communication will still matter, perhaps even more so, as a differentiator in a digitally saturated world.

Leading Gen Alpha Well

This generation will challenge leaders to evolve, not lower standards. What I expect will work:

- Clear roles and feedback loops
- Shorter planning cycles with visible outcomes
- Opportunities to build, test, and improve
- Mentorship that flows in both directions

What likely won't work with Gen Alpha:

- Fear-based narratives
- Stereotypes disguised as wisdom
- Assuming maturity without teaching it
- Confusing flexibility with a lack of accountability

Every generation improves the workplace when leaders meet them with curiosity instead of criticism.

A Leadership Opportunity

Gen Alpha is not a problem to solve. They are a responsibility to prepare for. They will inherit workplaces shaped by today's choices, our communication norms, leadership habits, and willingness to adapt. If Gen Alpha enters work environments that value clarity, trust, and contribution, they will meet those expectations.

And if history is any guide, they will raise the bar again.

Next, we'll turn our attention to **communication tips for new and emerging leaders**, many of whom are already stepping into responsibility.

CHAPTER 29. BE AN EFFECTIVE NEW LEADER

Leading when you're young, new, or inexperienced comes with a unique challenge: you may have authority before you have shared history. Your role isn't just to manage work, it's to earn trust, establish credibility, and set the tone for how work gets done.

As a leader, your responsibilities fall into three areas: your team, the work, and yourself. Strong leaders stay flexible, adjusting how they show up depending on the situation. The following strategies focus on what helps most when you're still building confidence, relationships, and perspective.

Respect Their Experience

If you're stepping into leadership for the first time, start by observing. You don't need to prove yourself on day one; you need to understand the environment you've inherited. Honor the experience of others by asking thoughtful, open-ended questions:

- "Can you describe what success has looked like in this role before?"
- "What's worked well here, and what hasn't?"
- "If I were doing an ideal job six months from now, what would you expect to see?"

You've already learned the power of listening and asking better questions. This is where those skills matter most. Early curiosity builds credibility faster than early change.

Set expectations for communication early. Ask about preferred cadence and channels. Some people want quick check-ins; others prefer fewer, more intentional conversations.

Give Them Room

One of the fastest ways to lose trust is to confuse leadership with constant oversight. Different generations and different personalities have different needs around autonomy and visibility. Highly independent employees may interpret frequent check-ins as a sign of mistrust. Others see them as support.

This isn't about right or wrong. It's about outcomes. When people feel trusted, they tend to take more ownership. When they feel monitored, they tend to disengage. Your job is to calibrate:

- What needs visibility?
- What needs freedom?
- Where does accountability actually add value?.

Don't Ignore Senior Staff

New leaders sometimes avoid addressing issues with seasoned employees, assuming they'll "age out" or that it's not worth the discomfort. The consequence of this choice is rarely neutral.

When standards are applied unevenly, the rest of the team notices. Over time, this erodes trust not just in the individual but also in you as a leader. Address behavior consistently. Clear expectations signal respect.

Implement Changes Deliberately

Once you've listened, observed, and built rapport, it's time to move forward. Change doesn't require force; it requires clarity and momentum. Before implementing something new:

- Clarify the long-term vision
- Involve the team where appropriate
- Share the "why" before the "how"

Ask how others would approach achieving the goal. Publish the plan. Then move with purpose.

Break large initiatives into manageable steps. Put actions on a timeline. **Treat goals like events, planned, prepared for, and followed up on.** Progress builds confidence, especially when you're still establishing your leadership rhythm.

Motivate and Appreciate on *Their* Terms

Appreciation isn't optional; it's a retention strategy. As a leader, how you recognize effort carries more weight than peer-to-peer praise. People want to know their work matters and that it's seen.

You've already learned how to give feedback and compliments. Apply those skills intentionally here. Notice what motivates each person. Some value public recognition; others prefer private acknowledgment. Some want growth opportunities; others want flexibility.

Esteem matters. When people feel respected and capable, they contribute more fully and stay longer.

Lead Forward

Being a young or new leader doesn't mean you lack influence. It means you're building it in real time. Stay curious. Stay consistent. Model the behavior you expect. Leadership credibility isn't granted; it's earned through everyday choices.

Now that we've explored how to work across generations, let's add another important layer to communication: understanding how gender influences expectations, perception, and interaction at work.

SECTION 7: GENDER-INCLUSIVE COMMUNICATION

CHAPTER 30. COMMUNICATE BEYOND GENDER STEREOTYPES

A white, middle-aged man said:

> "People need to be less sensitive."

This was his response when I explained why calling women at work "girl," "honey," "sweetie," or other diminutives isn't okay.

At the time, I didn't have the language I do now. Later, I read *35 Dumb Things Well-Intended People Say* by Dr. Maura Cullen, and one concept stuck with me: the Piling-On Principle.[7]

Piling on is like stubbing your toe first thing in the morning. No one *means* to hurt you, but all day long, people keep bumping it, stepping on it, and dropping things on it. Each moment, taken alone, might seem insignificant. Together, they hurt.

This is why impact doesn't care about intent. Whether someone meant harm or not, the effect is real and cumulative. It's hard to be less sensitive when someone is repeatedly hurt. And we don't get to choose what does or doesn't hurt other people.

A Personal Lesson in Language

In my late teens and early twenties, I managed the office for a service company. At the end of the day, I'd brief the evening staff, women old enough to be my grandmother, on appointments and priorities. One afternoon, I called out, "Okay, girls!" to get their attention.

Afterward, the owner pulled me aside. Calmly, she explained that calling experienced women "girls" minimized their authority and dismissed their experience. She was right. I didn't mean harm, but the impact mattered. I was piling on without realizing it.

That moment shaped how I think about communication at work. **Good intentions don't erase unintended consequences. Awareness reduces them.**

How Gender Stereotypes Show Up at Work

Stereotypes simplify people. They make communication seem easier in the short term, but far less effective in the long term. Both women and men experience this.

Common Stereotypes Women Encounter

Sex Object
Many women have experienced unwanted comments, attention, or behavior at work. When I've asked rooms full of women whether they've been harassed on the job, nearly every hand goes up. That reality shapes how language and behavior land.

Mother
Women are often expected to manage emotional labor, soothing conflict, planning events, and supporting others, regardless of role or workload.

Child
Sometimes framed as "protection," this stereotype limits women's access to risk, challenge, and high-visibility opportunities.

Iron Maiden
When women are direct or decisive, they may be labeled harsh or demanding, while the same behavior in men is praised as leadership.

Common Stereotypes Men Encounter

Men face stereotypes too, and they come with real costs.

The Fighter
Men are often expected to be aggressive, competitive, and always "on." Wanting flexibility or time with family can be perceived as a weakness or a lack of commitment.

The Stoic
Many men are taught not to ask for help, express doubt, or admit struggle. This limits collaboration and support.

The Breadwinner
Tying self-worth to income or job title creates pressure that becomes especially heavy during economic downturns or career transitions.

I've worked with men who stayed silent about harassment, burnout, or unfair treatment, because they feared ridicule, disbelief, or retaliation. Simplified statistics don't tell the whole story, but one thing is clear: underreporting is common, and silence is costly.

Notice the Pattern, Interrupt the Moment

This work isn't about perfection. It's about paying attention. Notice when:

- Language diminishes authority ("girl," "man up," "boys will be boys").

- Assumptions creep in about ambition, caregiving, toughness, or emotional capacity.
- Certain people consistently absorb more emotional labor or more risk.

Then interrupt gently:

- Use names and titles that reflect respect.
- Offer opportunity before protection.
- Normalize asking for help and learning out loud.
- Focus feedback on behavior, not identity.

These small shifts compound.

Shared Responsibility. Shared Benefit.

This isn't a women's issue or a men's issue. It's a workplace communication issue. When we reduce stereotyping:

- Trust increases.
- Feedback improves.
- Collaboration strengthens.
- Performance rises.

Try this:

- Whoever drinks the coffee makes it.
- Whoever dirties the dishes cleans them.
- Everyone says good morning.
- Everyone is eligible for stretch work.
- Everyone helps set the tone.

Respectful communication doesn't limit us. It frees us to work better together.

In the next chapter, we'll focus less on categories and more on how to communicate inclusively across differences, regardless of gender presentation, so that awareness turns into skill, and intention turns into impact.

CHAPTER 31. COMMUNICATE INCLUSIVELY ACROSS GENDERS

This chapter is about communicating effectively and respectfully at work across differences so your message lands as intended. You don't need perfect language. You do need **awareness, adaptability, and professionalism.**

Start with a Simple Principle

People differ in how they experience and present gender. That reality shows up in today's workplaces. Inclusive communication isn't about labels; it's about **avoiding unnecessary harm and keeping the focus on the work.**

Choose Words That Don't Exclude

Language shapes perception. When terms are gendered unnecessarily, people may feel overlooked or silently dismissed.

Instead of:

- "businessmen"
- "man-hours"
- "chairman"
- "man to man"

Use:

- "businesspeople"
- "work hours"
- "chair" or "chairperson"
- "face-to-face"

These substitutions aren't political. They're practical. They make communication clearer and more accurate.

Use Role Titles That Match the Work

Many roles were historically gendered. Updating titles reflects reality, not trendiness.

- Firefighter, not fireman
- Police officer, not policeman

Avoid adding gender qualifiers where they aren't relevant:

- "woman doctor"
- "male nurse"
- "female prosecutor"

These phrases unintentionally signal that one version of the role is the default and the other is an exception.

Write Policies That Focus on Behavior, Not Gender

Inclusive communication doesn't need gender labels. For example:

> "**Whoever** attains 15% greater sales than quota will have **their** commission increased the following year."

This removes unnecessary gender markers and improves readability. Many modern style guides accept **singular "they"** as grammatically correct. Using it keeps documents clear.

Avoid Assumptions

Assumptions often sneak in through humor, shorthand, or small talk.

- Don't guess someone's role at home.
- Don't assume orientation, identity, or preferences.
- Avoid jokes that rely on gender or sexuality for effect.

What feels casual to one person can feel risky or exclusionary to another, especially in professional settings.

When You're Unsure, Default to Curiosity

You won't get everything right. No one does. If you misspeak:

- A brief correction is enough.
- A genuine apology works.
- Overexplaining often makes things worse.

Inclusive communication isn't about walking on eggshells. It's about **paying attention and adjusting when needed**.

The Throughline

You've now explored how stereotypes form, how impact accumulates, and how language influences trust. The following section builds on this foundation, moving from awareness to influence by focusing on leadership-level communication. Whether you manage people formally or lead through example, the skills ahead will help you communicate with confidence, credibility, and care.

SECTION 8: LEADERSHIP LEVEL COMMUNICATION

CHAPTER 32. FIRST, KNOW THYSELF

Before you influence others, lead a team, or represent an organization, you need internal alignment.

Pressure at work has a way of pulling people out of themselves. Expectations creep in. Incentives distort decisions. Over time, it's easy to find yourself bending not because you lack integrity, but because you never paused to define what you would hold steady when the pressure was strongest. This chapter is about deciding who you are *before* you are tested.

Not who you think you should be.
Not who your boss wants you to be.
Not who the market rewards in the moment.

Who *you* are—so your external actions match your internal compass.

A Sovereign Nation of One

You are a sovereign nation of one. That means you govern yourself.

Take a moment to define your **personal sovereignty**, the non-negotiables that guide your decisions when things get complicated. These are not aspirational slogans. They are boundaries you are willing to live with, even when there is a cost.

Write them down. Sign and date the list. Revisit it when you feel tempted to compromise. Your list might include:

- *I will not lie for my boss.*
- *I will not accept "voluntary" overtime when my children are home.*
- *I will not stay silent when something violates my values.*

When these decisions are made in advance, they stop feeling dramatic. You're not reacting, you're executing a choice you already made.

This list is for you. It can evolve. It does not need to impress anyone or be seen by anyone else. Take some time to write it now.

Define Your Dream or Direction

What direction do you want your life and work to move in?
You don't need a five-year plan. You need a heading.

When you stare out the window or zone out in a meeting, what do you imagine doing differently? What work energizes you instead of draining you? What problems do you naturally want to solve?

- Who do you want to be known as?
- What do you want your name to be associated with?
- What kind of work feels honest for you right now?

Are You Aligned or Just Busy?

Alignment is where values meet behavior. Ask yourself:

- Does what I'm doing now support where I want to go?
- Am I gaining skills that move me closer to my direction?
- Is there a small way to test this next step without blowing up my life?

If you work in accounting but want to be a writer, can you contribute to the company blog? If you want to lead, can you mentor, train, or facilitate before you manage? Alignment doesn't require a leap. It requires intention.

Your External Presence Should Match Your Internal Clarity

Once you know who you are and where you're heading, your external presence should reinforce that story. Your reputation already exists. The question is whether it accurately reflects who you are.

Google yourself. See what others see. Remove anything that no longer represents who you are becoming. Remember: recruiters, leaders, collaborators, and volunteer boards will look you up long before they ask you questions.

Create professional profiles that reflect your direction:

- Use a current, professional photo.
- Write a clear bio that highlights what you do *and* how you think.

- Document accomplishments you're proud of.

Your digital presence should act as a quiet assistant, doing the explaining before you enter the room.

Why This Matters for What's Next

Internal alignment makes leadership communication possible. If you know your boundaries, you can hold others accountable. If you know your values, you can create psychological safety. If you respect yourself, you're far more likely to respect others.

The chapters ahead build on this foundation, moving from self-clarity to influence, accountability, and leadership-level communication.

Before you speak for others, lead others, or correct others, you must first be anchored in yourself. That's where effective leadership begins.

CHAPTER 33. HOLD OTHERS ACCOUNTABLE

Most of us work with someone we find difficult. And often, no one holds that person accountable, not because the behavior is acceptable, but because it feels risky. Sometimes that person even advances because they behave badly. Accountability can feel dangerous. But it is a skill that can be learned.

Why We Avoid Accountability Conversations

Under stress, many of us freeze. We let people cut in line, turn work in late, miss deadlines, or behave poorly. We tell ourselves it's safer to stay quiet. That it's "not that bad." That someone else will deal with it.

But silence has a cost.

When we don't speak up, our conscience often doesn't let it go. Passive avoidance can manifest physically as lost sleep, tension, or digestive issues, or emotionally as resentment and burnout. Avoiding accountability doesn't eliminate discomfort. It simply moves it.

Should I Address This?

You've seen this framework before, but it's worth repeating because accountability is where communication gets real. Ask yourself:

- Can I truly forgive and forget? Let it go permanently?
- Will this behavior likely happen again?
- Does it cost time, money, trust, or credibility?
- Does it affect customers, coworkers, or safety?

If the answer is yes and you can't genuinely let it go, it's time to talk. If you won't work with the person again and the issue won't resurface, you may choose not to engage.

Timing and Framing Matter

Don't confront in the heat of the moment. Take time to identify the real issue, not just what's easiest to point out. Address what matters, not what's convenient. Before the conversation, consider:

- How might this land from their perspective?
- What shared goal can I anchor this to?
- How can I make the conversation feel safe?

People hear accountability best when they understand the *why* behind it.

Be Direct, Early, and Clear

The first occurrence is often the easiest moment to address behavior. Describe what happened. State what you expect going forward. Keep it factual and private.

If it happens again, the issue has shifted. Now it's about reliability. You might say:

"This is the second time this has happened. You agreed it wouldn't. I'm concerned about my ability to rely on you."

This isn't punishment. It's information.

When Something "Comes Up"

Something will always come up. The issue isn't disruption; it's silence. Broken promises erode trust far faster than bad news delivered early. **Make it clear that you value transparency over perfection.** Try this:

"If something comes up, please tell me as soon as possible."

This sets a standard without shaming. It communicates that accountability includes communication, not just outcomes.

The Broken Record Test

If you're having the same accountability conversation repeatedly, one of two things is happening:

1. The person is unwilling or unable to change, or
2. You're addressing symptoms instead of the real issue.

Decide which it is before continuing. Accountability works when expectations are clear, consequences are consistent, and communication adapts to the audience. Leaders don't repeat themselves endlessly; they adjust.

Why This Matters

Accountability is not about control. It's about trust, predictability, and respect. When done well, it creates healthier teams, clearer expectations, and fewer surprises. When avoided, it breeds resentment and dysfunction. Effective leaders don't default to confrontation, but they don't avoid it either.

Next, we'll look at how leaders flex their communication style to meet people where they are and still move work forward.

CHAPTER 34. FLEX YOUR STYLE

Effective communication isn't about what you say. It's about how the other person receives it.

Two people can hear the same message and walk away with entirely different interpretations. That's why strong communicators don't just focus on clarity; they focus on *fit*. They ask, *How does this person best take in information?* and then adjust just enough to be understood.

Flexing your communication style isn't about changing who you are. It's about increasing the odds that your message lands the way you intend.

What Flexing Really Means

Style-flexers observe patterns, preferences, and context before deciding how to respond. This doesn't mean stereotyping; it means noticing signals and staying curious. Flexing is less about labels and more about awareness. Instead of asking, *What category does this person fall into?* ask:

- *What do they seem to value in communication?*
- *What pace are they comfortable with?*
- *How much context do they want before making a decision?*

Three Lenses That Shape How Messages Land

You don't need to analyze everything at once. Most communication differences fall into a few broad areas:

Context
Culture, organizational norms, and power dynamics shape expectations. Some people expect you to "read the air." Others prefer things spelled out clearly. Communication up the org chart often requires brevity; communication down or across may require detail.

Preference
Some people are task-oriented and want the facts quickly. Others are relationship-oriented and want connection first. Some think out loud. Others need time to process. These preferences can shift depending on stress, stakes, or timing.

Medium
How someone prefers to receive information matters. Email, phone, text, face-to-face, and video: none are inherently better, but mismatches can create friction. When in doubt, start with clarity and ask what works best.

Adjusting Without Overcorrecting

Flexing doesn't mean mirroring every behavior or walking on eggshells. You don't need to abandon your personality or values to communicate well. **Start by being yourself. Then make small adjustments.**

If someone speaks softly, lower your volume a notch. If they prefer summaries, lead with the headline. If they open with a personal connection, don't jump straight to the task.

When my mom taught me to drive, she warned me not to jerk the steering wheel. Minor corrections keep you in your lane. Overreacting only makes things worse. Communication works the same way.

When You're Not Sure What to Do

Err on the side of clarity and respect. If you're unsure how formal to be, choose slightly more formal. If you're unsure how much detail to give, ask. If you're unsure whether someone wants input or direction, check in before assuming.

Why This Matters

When people feel understood, they're more open. When communication feels safe, accountability becomes easier. Feedback lands better. Conflict de-escalates faster. Flexing your style isn't just a communication skill; it's a trust-building skill. And trust is the foundation of psychological safety.

Next, we'll look at how leaders and teams can intentionally create environments where people feel safe to speak up, ask questions, and do their best work because even the best communication strategies fail in unsafe workplaces.

CHAPTER 35. CREATE A SAFE AND HEALTHY WORKPLACE

A healthy employee is a productive employee. People do their best work when they feel safe enough to speak honestly, ask for help, and take reasonable risks.

Employees don't leave their personal lives at the door. Stress, uncertainty, and fear show up in how people communicate. When someone doesn't feel safe, they get defensive. They stop offering ideas. They avoid feedback. And if leaders don't know what's really happening, they can't fix what's broken. A safe workplace isn't soft. It's functional.

Safety as Communication Infrastructure

Psychological and emotional safety are the foundation of effective communication. When people feel safe, information flows. When they don't, it bottlenecks.

Safety doesn't mean everyone agrees. It means people can disagree without fear of humiliation, retaliation, or being written off. It means feedback travels in both directions and problems surface early.

Open Communication Builds Trust

Trust is built through a pattern of truth and promises kept. **When leaders consistently tell the truth and follow through, they earn credibility. In those environments, people don't just say what the boss wants to hear. They raise concerns, flag risks, and point out obstacles before time and money are wasted.** That kind of honesty saves organizations.

*A note about "truth": there isn't a single, objective version we all access equally. Our experiences, roles, and perspectives shape how we interpret events, like referees standing on different sides of the field. Self-aware communicators recognize this and speak with both clarity and tact. Saying "based on my experience" or "the way I see it" keeps conversations open rather than combative.

Truthful doesn't have to mean blunt. And tact doesn't mean avoidance.

Promises Matter More Than Speeches

A trustworthy leader:

- Delivers on commitments and communicates early when they can't
- Gives credit where it's due
- Avoids gossip
- Provides clear, timely feedback
- Thinks carefully before making promises

They don't need to preface statements with "honestly." Their consistency does that for them.

Reducing an "us versus them" dynamic is essential. Make shared goals and frame deadlines within the larger mission. Celebrate wins publicly. Address setbacks without blame. When people see how their work connects to the whole, trust increases, and so does accountability.

What a Healthy Workplace Looks Like

If you asked your team to draw a picture of a healthy workplace, what would they sketch? It wouldn't look identical for everyone, but one thing would be consistent: strong relationships. People want to feel respected, useful, and aligned.

Look at your organization's mission and values. Then look at your own. Where do they overlap? Start there. When people pull in the same direction, the organization moves further with less friction.

Emotional Safety Is a Leadership Skill

Emotional safety comes from feeling valued and respected. Communication creates safety, and safety improves communication. High pressure threatens that balance.

Aggression, intimidation, and chronic micromanagement erode safety quickly. So does ignoring concerns or, subtly or overtly, punishing people for speaking up. Leaders set the tone. Model the behavior you want to see:

- Thank people who raise issues the right way, even when it's inconvenient
- Be curious before defensive
- Show that disagreement doesn't equal disloyalty

You don't have to agree to make someone feel heard.

Make Respect Routine

Safety improves when speaking up becomes the norm rather than the exception. In one-to-one meetings, ask specific questions, not just "How's it going?" In team settings, dedicate time to concerns and rotate who brings them forward. This reinforces that surfacing issues is everyone's responsibility, not a personal risk.

Encourage collaboration where it makes sense. Pair people across functions or skill sets, not just departments. Breaking silos reduces misunderstandings and builds trust.

Physical and Mental Health Signals

You don't need a gym or a wellness budget to signal care. Small choices can contribute to a safe and healthy workplace. Try:

- Walking meetings
- Flexible spaces
- Reasonable expectations around availability

Mental health deserves the same seriousness. Harassment and bullying should never be tolerated. If the organization doesn't have a clear policy, make it your own standard. **People watch what leaders ignore as closely as what they enforce.**

Why This Matters

Safe workplaces don't happen by accident (pun intended). They're built through daily choices: what leaders say, what they follow up on, and what they allow to slide.

When people feel safe, communication improves. When communication improves, trust grows. And when trust grows, everything else becomes easier, from feedback and accountability to collaboration and performance.

One of the simplest ways to reinforce safety is also one of the most overlooked: showing appreciation. Let's look at how to do that well.

CHAPTER 36. SHOW APPRECIATION ON THEIR TERMS

We can't expect people to give their best if they don't feel seen or valued. Most leaders *believe* they show appreciation. The disconnect occurs when appreciation is delivered in a way that matters to the giver but not to the receiver. Appreciation only works when it lands.

Start With "Thank You"

A foundry worker once asked me (genuinely puzzled):

> "Why do some people need to be thanked all the time just for doing their job?"

It was a fair question and a revealing one. That comment reminded me how easy it is to assume our preferences are universal. For some people, hearing "thank you" regularly is essential. For others, words alone don't register unless they're paired with opportunity, flexibility, or pay. The good news? Saying thank you is easy and costs nothing.

Your team invests time, energy, and effort every day. A simple, specific thank-you reinforces that their work matters. Make it a habit to thank someone daily.

Personal notes are especially powerful. If someone came through in a crunch or helped make a project successful, write it down. (See Chapter 7 for tips on sending notes.)

If someone goes out of their way to help a client, close a deal, or contribute beyond their role, email both the individual and their supervisor. Recognition carries more weight when it travels upward.

Acts of Appreciation Matter, Too

Some people feel valued more through action than through words. **Create a culture where kindness is visible:**

- Bring in a treat
- Highlight an employee each month
- Give your most valuable resource, your attention
- Ask for advice, and actually listen

Small gestures matter. If someone's been eyeing a better chair, give it to them. If the weather's perfect and the week's been heavy, consider a Friday afternoon off. Invite families to a casual picnic. These moments build goodwill that no policy can manufacture.

Fairness Is a Form of Appreciation

Appreciation isn't only expressed through praise or rewards. It's also communicated through fairness.

Pay, promotions, flexibility, and accountability all signal what an organization truly values. When decisions feel inconsistent or unexplained, appreciation loses credibility. When difficult calls are made, explaining how they align with stated values and long-term goals reinforces trust.

For employees from historically marginalized groups, a single instance of perceived inequity, unequal pay, inconsistent standards, or favoritism can undo years of goodwill. Fairness is one of the clearest ways people decide whether they are genuinely valued.

Invest in Growth

People don't just leave companies; they leave ceilings. Investing in development signals belief. Share the company vision. Help people see how their role connects to what's next.

If you see leadership potential, invite them into rooms they haven't been in yet. Send them to conferences. Support their desire to take classes. Cover tuition when possible.

Recognize Milestones Thoughtfully

Tenure still matters. Acknowledge work anniversaries. Ask how people prefer to be recognized. Some enjoy public praise; others prefer a quiet thank-you. Don't guess, ask.

When giving gifts, practicality usually wins. Gas cards, coffee gift cards, time off, or services like house or car cleaning are often more appreciated than branded items. If you do give swag, make it something people actually want to use.

Appreciation Includes Giving Back

Recognize contributions beyond the job. If someone volunteers, mentors, creates art, or gives back in meaningful ways, ask if you can share the good news. Celebrate sustainability wins. Host a bring-your-child-to-work day. Offer paid volunteer time employees can use however they choose.

These signals say: *We value who you are, not just what you produce.*

Appreciate with Pay

Here's the minimum: Compensation has to meet basic needs. Pay also needs to be competitive enough that leaving isn't the obvious solution.

For some, pay-for-performance is the clearest form of appreciation. While younger generations often say flexibility and purpose matter more than money, they still want to be evaluated and rewarded based on merit.

Strong compensation plans balance short- and long-term incentives. They reward results, promote retention, and align individual effort with organizational goals.

Why Appreciation Matters

Appreciated employees don't just stay longer. They speak better of the organization. They refer others. They defend the brand when it's criticized. When people feel valued on *their* terms, they don't just do the work; they proudly represent the company they work for. And that's how employees become ambassadors.

CHAPTER 37. ENCOURAGE BRAND ADVOCACY

Happy customers and engaged employees talk. The question isn't *whether* people are talking about your organization, it's whether they're saying what you hope they'll say.

Brand advocacy happens when people genuinely believe in what you're doing and choose to share it. Your role is not to script them, but to create the conditions that make advocacy natural.

What Is a Brand Advocate?

A **brand advocate** is someone, often an employee, customer, or partner, who voluntarily speaks positively about an organization based on real experience.

A **brand ambassador**, on the other hand, is typically a formal role. Ambassadors are asked (and often paid) to represent a brand and promote its products or services. They are expected to align with the organization's values, voice, and standards.

Why Are You in Business?

I've never met an entrepreneur who started a business *only* to make money. There's always something more, a problem to solve, a gap to fill, a better way to do things. Brand advocacy starts there, with clarity at the top. Do people know why your organization exists beyond revenue? Can they articulate it in their own words?

If you lead a department, team, or project, the same principle applies. What are you building? What do you stand for? What problem are you committed to solving? When people believe in the *why*, they'll help carry the message, often more credibly than you ever could alone.

Let Others Say It for You

People trust third-party voices more than self-promotion. That's why influence is so powerful.

Rather than broadcasting louder, effective communicators focus on **amplifying through relationships**. Here's a simple, repeatable framework that works across marketing, leadership, recruiting, and internal communication.

Three Steps to Leverage Influence

1. Know More

Start with a clear understanding of the audience you want to reach. Demographics matter, but go deeper. What do they value? What frustrates them? What motivates their decisions? When you understand both *who* your audience is and *why* they care, your message becomes relevant instead of generic.

2. Get Closer

Influence grows with proximity. Identify the people your audience already listens to, both inside and outside your organization. These might be industry peers, respected employees, long-term customers, or trusted connectors.

Pay attention to what motivates them. Do achievement, ideals, or self-expression drive them? The closer you get to understanding their perspective, the easier it becomes to communicate in a way that resonates.

3. Emotionally Connect

People don't advocate for ideas; they advocate for relationships. Connection takes time. It may look like a thoughtful follow-up, a one-to-one conversation, or simply showing genuine curiosity about someone else's work and priorities.

Ask good questions. Listen carefully. Build trust before you ask for anything. When people feel seen, respected, and aligned with your mission, advocacy follows naturally.

Advocacy Is Not a Campaign

This process isn't limited to marketing. It applies to leadership, sales, employee engagement, and recruitment. Knowing more, getting closer, and connecting emotionally help people feel confident saying "yes" and comfortable sharing that decision with others.

As we move into persuasive communication, keep this framework in mind. Influence isn't about pressure. It's about clarity, credibility, and connection.

SECTION 9: PERSUASIVE COMMUNICATION

CHAPTER 38. GET PEOPLE TO SAY, "YES!"

If you want people to say yes, start by listening. Persuasion is not about pressure. It's about understanding. When people feel heard, respected, and safe, they're far more open to new ideas.

Listen First

Listening is a two-step process. First, do your homework. Research the person or audience you're trying to persuade. If it's an individual, review their LinkedIn profile or website. If it's a group, understand what they value, what pressures they face, and what success looks like to them. It's always easier to persuade someone when you know their context.

Second, be fully present when you meet. Give them your attention. Use culturally appropriate eye contact. Use their name. Don't interrupt. (If you need a refresher on first impressions and presence, head back to Section 1.)

Good listeners are curious. They ask open-ended questions and listen for what matters most. Apply the principles from the previous chapter: **Know more. Get closer. Emotionally connect.**

Present the Whole Picture

Credibility grows when you're honest. Present both the advantages and the limitations of what you're proposing. Transparency builds trust.

Keep the focus on *them*, not you. Use their language. Show how your idea solves a real problem or makes their work easier. Avoid jargon and technical detail unless you know it serves your audience. Structure matters. A strong presentation includes:

- A clear hook
- A concise introduction
- Three or four supporting points
- A confident close

Bring Appropriate Energy

You don't need to be flashy, but you do need to care. People are persuaded by conviction, not just volume. If you believe in your idea, let that belief show calmly and confidently. Genuine enthusiasm sparks curiosity and lowers resistance.

Use Assertive, Respectful Body Language

Your body often speaks before you do. Stand or sit with an open posture. Avoid crossed arms or pointed fingers. Keep your gestures relaxed and intentional. Match your delivery to your audience while still honoring your point of view.

Use Your Voice Well

Clarity persuades. Speak at a measured pace. Pause instead of filling space with "ums" and "ahs." Silence can be powerful. Plan your key points and deliver them with intention.

Tell a Story

Stories persuade because they connect ideas to emotion. Some people decide with data. Many decide with narrative. The most effective communicators use both.

For years, my parents had a booth at the Wisconsin State Fair next to Vita-Mix. These are expensive blenders. Most people don't buy one without seeing it in action.

The demonstrators didn't just list features: motor speed, warranty, and durability. They told stories. Someone brought in a blender that their grandmother had owned for decades. Another customer shared how making smoothies helped them change their health. Facts informed. Stories convinced.

Use Relevant Examples

Case studies and examples help people imagine success. Choose examples your audience can relate to. Tie each one back to your main point. Include numbers when appropriate, but don't drown the message in data.

Invite and Handle Questions Well

Instead of asking, "Do you have any questions?" try, "What questions do you have?"

Thank people for their questions. Repeat them to ensure clarity and to give yourself time to think. Consider what's behind the question: concern, curiosity, or risk. If you don't know the answer, say so. Write it down. Follow up. Trust grows when people see that you take their questions seriously.

Lead with Empathy

You can't fix every problem, but you can acknowledge it. Try to understand their perspective and constraints. Avoid saying, "I know exactly how you feel." You don't. Empathy doesn't require sameness; it requires attention.

End with a Clear Next Step

Don't leave people guessing. A strong presentation naturally leads to action, but you still need to name it. Be clear. Be direct. Ask them to decide, call, click, approve, or try the next step.

The most durable, yes, is the one people choose for themselves. Consultative communication respects autonomy, invites dialogue, and treats others as capable partners. It shifts influence from persuasion to alignment. Next, we'll explore consultative communication, how to ask the right questions, slow the conversation down, and help others think their way forward.

CHAPTER 39. COMMUNICATE CONSULTATIVELY

Some of the best decisions I've seen weren't made by the person with the title. They were shaped by the people closest to the work, the ones who saw problems early, understood constraints, and knew what would actually succeed in the real world. Consultative communication creates space for those voices.

This approach is especially valuable in diverse, high-performing organizations that hire for perspective rather than sameness. It develops leaders, increases ownership, and works even without formal authority. When people feel genuinely heard before decisions are made, morale and results improve.

What Is Consultative Communication?

Consultative communication uses open-ended questions to surface perspectives, uncover blind spots, and identify underlying concerns before decisions are finalized. The signal is simple but powerful: *input is welcome before decisions are made.*

This approach remains task-focused while honoring the relationship between the leader and the employee. It requires humility: a willingness to listen, consider differing viewpoints, and resist the urge to decide alone simply because you can.

At its best, consultative communication creates win-win outcomes. Employees gain confidence and ownership, and leaders make more informed, resilient decisions.

Why Use a Consultative Approach?

Consultative communication:

- Builds trust and credibility
- Clarifies goals and expectations
- Increases buy-in during change
- Surfaces risks earlier
- Develops critical thinking and future leaders

It reassures employees who may doubt their ability and engages those closest to the work, those with the clearest view of what's really happening.

When Is Consultative Communication Most Effective?

Consultative communication is most useful when:

- You don't have the full picture
- Frontline employees hold key knowledge
- You want shared ownership, not silent compliance
- You're navigating change or resistance
- You want to develop people, not just get tasks done

It does take time. There will be moments when discussions feel messy or when a resident "devil's advocate" dominates. That doesn't mean the approach isn't working; it often means it's surfacing real issues.

Create the Conditions for Consultation

Consultative communication doesn't require consensus, but it does require safety. People won't offer honest input if they believe disagreement will be punished or ignored. Before asking for perspectives, leaders should consider what signals they're sending. An open culture isn't built solely through policies. It's built through daily behavior. Ask yourself:

- Do people see me respond calmly when something isn't working?
- Do I thank people for raising concerns even when I disagree?
- Do I invite input early, or only after decisions are mostly made?

Consultative leaders make it clear that speaking up is part of the job, not a personal risk. That doesn't mean every idea is adopted. It means ideas are heard, considered, and respected. Civil disagreement should be treated as a contribution, not defiance.

One of the strongest signals a leader can send is naming challenges themselves. When leaders say, *"This isn't working,"* **or** *"I may be missing something,"* **they lower the cost of honesty for everyone.**

Clarity also matters. If you're gathering ideas but will make the final call, say so. If you're seeking shared ownership, say that too. Ambiguity about decision-making authority can shut people down faster than disagreement. **The goal isn't to eliminate tension. It's to make it productive.**

How to Be a Consultative Communicator

If you've led primarily through direction, transitioning to a consultative style takes intention. Start small. Demonstrate curiosity. Be transparent about what input will influence and what won't.

If you've already been practicing honest feedback, accountability, and psychological safety, consultative communication will feel like a natural next step.

Facilitate with Intention

When facilitating consultative conversations:

- Design a clear agenda
- Pay attention to both content and group dynamics
- Keep the conversation moving toward its purpose
- Use varied formats to engage different communication styles
- Intervene when voices dominate, or others are dismissed

Strong facilitation protects candor without letting the conversation drift. Consultative communication isn't passive leadership. It's engaged leadership that listens deeply, decides thoughtfully, and brings people along with clarity.

Next, we'll look at empowering communication, how leaders can help others build confidence, take ownership, and act with intention, even without formal authority.

CHAPTER 40. EMPOWER THROUGH COMMUNICATION

Empowering communication isn't removing the guardrails. It's handing someone the map and trusting them to drive. When people understand what matters and why, they can make smart decisions without waiting for permission.

What Is It?

Cascadia Workshops, inspired by Marshall Rosenberg, PhD, describes Empowered Communication (also known as Compassionate or Nonviolent Communication™) as a way of speaking that supports understanding, cooperation, and shared problem-solving even in moments of disagreement.[8] At its core, empowering communication:

- Focuses on needs and values rather than blame or fear
- Encourages personal responsibility
- Supports cooperation over control
- Works even when others don't use the same approach

Rather than relying on guilt, pressure, or authority, this style builds goodwill and self-esteem. It assumes people want to contribute meaningfully when they feel safe and respected.

Why Communicate in an Empowering Way?

Empowered employees don't need policies for every scenario. They develop judgment. When leaders communicate in empowering ways:

- Decisions happen faster
- Micromanagement decreases
- Ownership increases
- Capacity multiplies

This approach is especially practical when delegating, navigating complexity, or when you don't have the bandwidth to control every detail.

Paired with consultative communication, empowerment creates teams that understand not just *what* they're doing, but *why* it matters. Frequent "ten-thousand-foot views" help employees think beyond tasks and develop an executive mindset.

Empowering leaders also recognize individual strengths. They don't try to make everyone the same. If you're unsure what motivates someone, ask:

"What would help you grow professionally right now?"

When Empowering Communication Is Most Useful

Empowering communication is particularly valuable when:

- Work requires independent judgment
- Employees hesitate out of fear of making mistakes
- You notice constant checking-in or decision paralysis
- Creativity or ownership has stalled

Some employees ask for direction at every step, not because they lack ability, but because they fear getting it wrong. Empowering communication replaces fear with guardrails. Instead of constant instructions, offer **clear boundaries**, then step back:

> "Here's what success looks like. If you stay within these parameters, use your judgment."

That message builds confidence and accountability.

Practical Ways to Empower Through Communication

Empowerment doesn't require grand gestures. It's often conveyed through small, consistent choices:

- **Invite ideas early**, not after decisions are made
- **Trust without hovering**
- **Delegate decision-making**, not just tasks
- **Reward thoughtful risk-taking**, even when outcomes aren't perfect
- **Develop others intentionally** through education and stretch opportunities
- **Acknowledge effort and progress**, not just results

Remove Barriers to Empowerment

Empowerment fails when communication is unclear. Avoid jargon. Match your language to your audience. Confirm understanding. Be concise. When change is coming, frame it with purpose and address concerns early.

Resistance is often a signal of uncertainty, lack of confidence, or unclear incentives. Empowering leaders reinforce that input is expected and valued, not risky. **Metatalk**, naming what's happening in the conversation, can help regulate tension:

> "I know this is a heavy conversation, and I appreciate your honesty."

Statements like this signal awareness and respect without judgment.

Structural barriers matter, too. Rigid approval processes or one-way communication can quietly undermine empowerment. Leaders should periodically examine how information actually flows, not just how it's supposed to.

Availability also matters. You don't need an open door at all times, but intentional access builds trust. Scheduled check-ins or drop-in hours communicate presence.

Empowerment Isn't Perfection

Even with skill and care, communication won't always land as intended. Misunderstandings happen. Emotions surface. Tension builds. What matters most isn't avoiding these moments; it's responding well when they occur.

In the next section, we'll explore what happens when communication breaks down and how effective leaders manage conflict without losing trust, credibility, or momentum.

SECTION 10: COMMUNICATION BREAKDOWNS

CHAPTER 41. MANAGE CONFLICT

Conflict is a natural and recurring part of work. It shows up when people with different priorities and perspectives try to solve problems together. That doesn't mean something is wrong. It means something is happening.

Do We Need Conflict?

No one *needs* conflict for its own sake. But trying to eliminate it is unrealistic and often counterproductive. Organizations that suppress disagreement also suppress innovation, improvement, and honest problem-solving.

Businesses evolve. Markets shift. Teams grow. Conflict is often a byproduct of growth. Learning to manage it well allows you to use it as a tool rather than letting it become a liability.

Some of us avoid conflict at all costs, others lean into it too hard, and most of us are somewhere in between. One of the most effective ways to manage conflict is to let it be part of everyday work life, address it early, handle it directly, and frame it constructively.

Frame It First

Framing conflict is the quiet skill underneath every effective response. Anxiety and excitement feel remarkably similar in the body. The same racing heart and heightened alertness show up in both. When you feel that surge, you get to choose the story you tell yourself.

> Instead of *I'm anxious about this*, try *I'm engaged and ready to solve something important.*

That shift alone often changes your tone, posture, and willingness to listen and engage thoughtfully.

What Well-Managed Conflict Makes Possible

When conflict is handled thoughtfully, several outcomes become more likely.

Clearer listening. Strong communicators don't enter conflict to win. They enter to understand. Active listening allows more information to surface and leads to better decisions.

Emotional regulation. Conflict creates an opportunity to practice self-control. Remaining calm, firm, and flexible builds credibility. When you manage yourself well, others are more likely to trust your intentions.

Professional differentiation. Conflict reveals how you show up under pressure. Can you engage respectfully with someone who disagrees with you? Handling tension well allows you to express your perspective without damaging relationships.

Stronger working relationships. When conflict is addressed directly and fairly, tension dissipates faster. Coworkers don't feel forced to take sides. Work continues without unnecessary friction, and trust has room to grow.

Greater clarity around needs and boundaries. Conflict often highlights what matters most. Friction clarifies limits. When you articulate your needs clearly, without apology, you teach others how to work with you more effectively.

Increased flexibility. Managing conflict well doesn't require being right. It requires being open. Flexibility signals confidence, not weakness. Leaders who can adjust their perspective are more likely to be seen as fair, grounded, and credible.

Problem-Solving, Not Problem Avoidance

The goal at work isn't to avoid problems; it's to solve them. Change is uncomfortable. Disagreement is inevitable. But when conflict is approached with discipline, analyzing the situation, discussing it openly, and agreeing on next steps, it becomes productive rather than disruptive.

Over time, this approach builds resilience. Teams move through challenges more quickly. Individuals gain confidence in their ability to navigate difficult conversations.

When Conflict Is Left Unmanaged

Unaddressed conflict rarely stays quiet. It shows up as sarcasm, passive aggression, gossip, or outright hostility. It wastes time and energy, increases stress, and erodes morale. Over time, it damages trust and productivity.

Conflict tests how well we listen, set boundaries, and take responsibility for our communication choices. When handled well, it strengthens clarity and trust. When mishandled, it exposes gaps in skill, awareness, or leadership.

The next chapter focuses on the moment of confrontation itself: what helps, what hurts, and which habits quietly escalate tension.

CHAPTER 42. CONFRONT WITH CLARITY

Confrontation is not about being right, winning, or unloading frustration. It's a communication choice, one that either restores clarity or creates collateral damage. This chapter offers practical options for addressing issues directly while preserving professionalism and working relationships. This kind of conversation usually comes after feedback has already been given and the issue hasn't changed.

Confrontation carries more risk than feedback. Emotions may already be involved, expectations may feel threatened, and trust may be strained. Language choices matter more here because the margin for error is smaller. That being said, there is no single "right" script. Different situations require different approaches. What matters most is intention and clarity.

Language That Escalates Tension

Some language almost guarantees defensiveness because the delivery shifts the focus from behavior to character. Phrases that tend to derail productive confrontation include:

- "You always…"
- "You never…"
- Threats (explicit or implied)
- Humor that minimizes the issue
- Physical contact offered without consent

These choices turn a conversation into a debate about fairness, tone, or intent, none of which resolve the original issue.

Language That Keeps the Conversation Productive

More effective confrontation centers on **impact and expectations**, not blame. Helpful framing often sounds like:

- "Here's what I'm noticing…"
- "This is the impact I'm experiencing…"
- "Help me understand what's happening from your side."

This language doesn't guarantee agreement, but it significantly increases the chance of being heard. Let's look at a few ways to confront someone.

Option One: The Clarifying Conversation

Not every issue requires a formal structure. In early-stage or lower-stakes situations, a clarifying conversation may be all that's needed. This approach is rooted in interest-based negotiation and psychological safety research.[9] It's useful when:

- You're unsure of the root cause
- You want to prevent a pattern from forming
- The relationship is collaborative

A clarifying conversation often sounds like this:

- *"I've noticed the deadline has shifted a few times."*
- *"That's making planning harder on my end."*
- *"What's getting in the way?"*
- *"What would help this stay on track?"*

This method invites ownership without accusation and often surfaces new information.

Option Two: The Four-Part Assertion Message

One reliable option for requesting a behavioral change is the four-part assertion message, widely used in assertiveness and interpersonal communication research.[10] It's especially useful when emotions are high or the issue has already occurred more than once. It follows a simple sequence:

Behavior → Feeling → Consequence → Request

1. **Behavior**
   Describe what you can observe, factually and specifically. Avoid speculation about motives.
   "Twice this week, you were late covering the phones during my lunch break."

2. **Feeling**
   Name your emotional response without blame. This keeps the message human rather than accusatory.
   "I'm frustrated."

3. **Consequence**
   Explain why it matters. This connects the behavior to real impact.
   "Because my lunch is shortened, I don't return refreshed, and it affects how I handle customers."

4. **Request**
   Clearly state what you want to happen next.
   "I need you to arrive on time, or I'll extend my lunch to ensure I receive the full break."

Option Three: Formal Escalation (When the Pattern Persists)

Sometimes clarity and goodwill aren't enough. **Formal escalation is not punishment; it's a boundary.** It's the appropriate next step when behavior continues despite clear, respectful attempts to address it. Formal escalation may be necessary when:

- The issue affects safety, legality, or compliance
- Commitments continue to be broken
- Power dynamics prevent resolution
- The behavior impacts others beyond you

Escalating well means being intentional, not reactive.

How to Escalate Professionally

- **Document facts**, not feelings. Dates, behaviors, outcomes.
- **Reference prior conversations** and what was agreed upon.
- **Follow established channels** (HR, leadership, policy).
- **State your goal**: resolution, not retaliation.
- **Remain consistent** in tone and message.

Escalation works best when it's framed as:

- *"I've tried to resolve this directly."*
- *"The issue is continuing."*
- *"Here's the documented impact."*
- *"I'm asking for support in resolving it."*

Handled this way, escalation protects everyone involved.

Choosing the Right Approach

Think of confrontation as a spectrum, not a switch. Each option assumes that earlier, lower-stakes conversations have failed to resolve the issue.

- **Clarifying conversation** when awareness may be the issue
- **Assertion message** when a boundary needs reinforcement
- **Formal escalation** only when patterns persist or stakes are high

Each choice carries consequences. Thoughtful communicators choose the lightest approach that still achieves clarity.

A Reminder

Clear confrontation is not unkind. Avoidance is not neutral. And professionalism doesn't require silence. Handled well, confrontation strengthens trust. Handled poorly, it creates fear and resentment. The difference is rarely *what* you say; it's *how* you say it.

Some situations, however, are less about skill and more about strategy. When patterns persist, or personalities complicate progress, communication alone may not be enough. Chapter 43 focuses on navigating difficult people at work.

CHAPTER 43. WORK PRODUCTIVELY WITH DIFFICULT PEOPLE

Every workplace has at least one difficult person. Sometimes that person is a peer. Sometimes it's a supervisor. At times, it's us.

Difficult behavior usually surfaces under pressure when needs go unmet, boundaries are unclear, or power dynamics are misused. That doesn't excuse poor behavior, but it does give us useful information. Understanding *why* someone is difficult helps us choose *how* to respond, rather than reacting on instinct.

In personal life, avoidance is often an option. At work, it rarely is. Learning to deal effectively with difficult people is not about fixing them; it's about managing yourself, protecting the work, and making intentional choices.

A Note on Labels

"Difficult" isn't a personality type. It's a pattern of behavior, often temporary, sometimes chronic, and frequently situational. Power matters here. A difficult coworker with little authority is different from a difficult leader who controls workload, evaluations, or advancement. There is no universal solution. What works depends on the behavior, the relationship, and the cost of engagement.

Start with Empathy (Without Excusing Behavior)

Empathy makes difficult interactions easier to navigate, not easier to tolerate. If you know someone personally, you may be able to complete the sentence: *"It must be difficult when..."* Divorce. Health issues. Financial pressure. Caregiving. Burnout.

You don't need to know their full story to recognize that stress often drives behavior. Empathy helps you stay grounded. It does **not** require you to accept disrespect, unpredictability, or harm.

Can You Ignore It?

Sometimes people ask this, hoping the answer is yes. If you can genuinely forgive, let go, and move forward without resentment, that's a valid choice. But unresolved tension rarely disappears on its own. More often, it leaks through as complaints, avoidance, or subtle disengagement.

Chronic venting can quietly brand you as "high-maintenance," even when your concerns are legitimate. That said, you don't need to be friends with everyone at work.

Boundaries are not avoidance. If reasonable, you may be able to:

- Limit unnecessary interaction
- Reduce optional collaboration
- Step back from voluntary committees
- Choose projects that don't require close alignment

When Tempers Flare

Safety comes first. Trust your instincts. If a situation feels unsafe, remove yourself. If you stay:

- Keep your voice low and steady
- Listen more than you speak

- Avoid telling someone to "calm down," model calm instead
- Maintain neutral body language
- Don't touch. Don't crowd. Don't escalate

Let them vent. Many people talk themselves down once they feel heard. Silence, patience, and steady presence are often more effective than rebuttals. If behavior crosses into verbal abuse or threats, disengage and document.

After the Moment

Once emotions settle, decide what's next. Sometimes that means a direct conversation. Sometimes it means involving a manager or HR. Sometimes it means adjusting boundaries. The right choice depends on the pattern, not just the incident. Document facts. Stick to behavior and impact. Avoid character judgments.

Are *You* the Difficult One?

Yes. At times, all of us are. Patterns are informative. If you consistently struggle with the same type of person or situation, it's worth asking why.

I know I tend to interrupt at work, especially on the phone. Awareness didn't change that overnight, but it helped me adapt. I slow down. I write questions down, so I'm not worried about forgetting my thoughts.

Find a trusted colleague or mentor and ask privately for honest feedback. Self-awareness makes you easier to work with.

Take Care of Yourself

Difficult interactions are draining. Step away when you can. Move your body. Call someone you trust. After a tough exchange, name one thing you handled well and one thing you'd adjust next time. This turns stress into skill.

Should You Leave Your Job?

Sometimes, difficult people make us want to quit our jobs. Should we? Sometimes.. But rarely impulsively. Changing jobs should be a **considered decision**, not an emotional reaction. Every workplace has friction. The real question is whether the situation is:

- Sharpening your skills or slowly wearing you down
- Isolated or systemic
- Temporary or unlikely to change

If the role still aligns with your values and growth goals, staying may build resilience and credibility. If the environment consistently violates your boundaries or well-being, it may be time to redirect your energy toward what's next. Leaving is not failure. Staying without reflection isn't a strength either. Both are choices.

Throughout this section, one idea remains consistent: communication is intentional. How you listen, respond, set boundaries, and decide when to stay or go shapes both your reputation and your long-term success.

The following section looks beyond individual interactions to how intentional communication supports sustainable leadership, influence, and career longevity.

SECTION 11: NEXT LEVEL COMMUNICATION

CHAPTER 44. KEEP YOURSELF MOTIVATED

We procrastinate for two common reasons: fear that our work won't be good enough or resistance to doing something uncomfortable. **The antidote to fear is focus.**

Name the outcome you're trying to avoid, then work backward. If you're worried your work won't meet the mark, define what *good enough* means. Create a short checklist. Work toward it.

Motivation is unreliable. Much of meaningful work is hard, dull, or inconvenient, and waiting for inspiration is a losing strategy. Progress comes from showing up anyway.

If–then planning can help. This simple technique prepares you for obstacles: *If* this happens, *then* I'll do that. It replaces hesitation with action.

If-Then Planning

If-then planning, also called implementation intention, is a planning strategy that successful leaders use. They identify what gets in the way of accomplishing a goal. Let's work through one.

Write down a current big goal.

What are your impulse triggers that prevent this goal? Brainstorm and write down whatever is standing in your way. When, what, or who is a roadblock?

Do you waste time on email or social media? Your if-then would be something like, "If I work on my hardest project for twenty minutes each morning, then I will check my email."

_____

_____

_____

Examples of If-Then Plans

- **If** I use screen time on my iPhone, **then** I can monitor how much time I spend on nonessential activities.
- **If** I leave my phone in the other room, **then** checking it will require physical activity.
- **If** a coworker is irritating me, **then** I will go for a brisk walk to get out my frustration.

Create a series of if-then plans for how you'll overcome each trigger.

_____

_____

_____

Goal Planning Tips for Success

- Choose one habit at a time.
- Set a specific, big-picture goal.
- Write it down on a piece of paper.

- Give yourself a firm start date and end date.
- Sign and date it.

Create mini goals to measure your progress and stay focused. Small successes help you stick to your plan. If you're working on time management, keep track of all your activities. This gives you a baseline to measure progress.

When changing habits, decide whether you will go cold turkey or find a replacement. Studies highlight the benefits of both methods. If you're trying to eat more healthful foods, eliminating one item (not an entire food category) may be advantageous.

What is your least favorite treat? If you can easily say no to chips or cookies, decide you'll never eat another one again. Once the decision is made, you may find there's no temptation. (Some people experience the opposite.)

On the other hand, a replacement could be a good distraction. For example, "**If** I feel like buying something on Amazon, **then** I will go for a walk instead."

If You Fail

I missed my first deadline for publishing this book. And the second one.

Failure happens.

Decide to learn from failure and move forward. If you miss a deadline or goal, brainstorm again. Add more ideas to your if-then plan. What caused the failure? Do I have another trigger I wasn't aware of? What can I do moving forward?

Decide *now* how you will respond to specific temptations. **It'll be easier to choose the path that aligns with your goals if you lay out your if-then plan in a moment of strength** rather than trying to figure it out in a moment of weakness.

Identify Self-Motivaters

Everyone holds different work values to feel satisfied and fulfilled. It could be an intellectual challenge, helping others, or independence that keeps us going. It might be money, fame, power, social interaction, or creative expression.

By understanding *your* career motivation, you can create an environment in which you will thrive. What motivates you?

Consider the following categories outlined by Carter McNamara of Authenticity Consulting.[11] **Rank them, starting with 1 as the highest motivator.** You might have several categories that rank a 1. Don't worry about getting your ranking perfect. Usually, your first answer is the best.

Rank these categories. Which is your top motivation?

__ Career Development/Success

__ Comfort/Relaxation

__ Health/Balance/Energy

__ Influence/Leadership

__ Learning/Knowledge/Discovery

__ Materials/Possessions

__ Recognition/Praise

___ Security/Money/Home

___ Social/Affiliation/Popularity/Acceptance

___ Status/Prestige/Stand Out/Reputation

___ Task Accomplishment/Problem Solving/Achievement

___ Teaching/Guiding Others

___ Vitality/Energy

___ Others? _____

What rewards motivate you (internal/external)? What kind of praise motivates you? What would help you (and maybe others) understand your motivation? Please take a moment to describe your thoughts.

_____

_____

_____

_____

_____

Motivation and procrastination don't exist in a vacuum. The habits and choices you make with yourself inevitably show up in how you work with others. Chapter 45 shifts the focus outward, examining how motivation, momentum, and follow-through are influenced by the people around you and how your communication affects theirs.

CHAPTER 45. MOTIVATE OTHERS

There is debate about whether it is possible to motivate another person. But we *can* determine what drives them and use that to our advantage. Be flexible, and you'll find your coworkers' or employees' motivations.

Intrinsic Versus Extrinsic Motivation

Extrinsic motivation (money, carrot and stick, fear) is short-lived. **Intrinsic motivation is more sustainable.** It supports who the person is and what they believe. Feeling valued and seeing the work as purposeful will keep employees motivated and engaged in the long term.

If organizations hire as much for values as they do for skills, they'll have happier, more intrinsically motivated employees.

Make your values visible. Don't just hang the mission statement on the wall. Live it. Incorporate it into your communications. Catch people living your values and celebrate them.

Five Ways to Incite Motivation

1. Build Relationships

People work for people. Be more than an email signature. Get to know your employees. Show them they are valued. When possible, check in face-to-face. Ask for input. Empower them with projects commensurate with their ability to implement good decisions.

2. Be an Example

You set the tone with your work ethic, attitude, and behavior. Show your excitement about projects and goals. Be optimistic. Expect the best, and they're likely to rise to meet your expectations.

Think about your favorite and least favorite boss. What made them so inspiring or challenging? List the qualities of your favorite and least favorite leaders. Compare them with your traits.

>Favorite

>Least Favorite

What do you want to embody? Which would you like to avoid? **Develop a strategy for becoming the leader you want to be.** Remember, you can't pour out yourself if your well is dry. Invest in yourself.

3. Praise

Recognition and sincere praise improve morale and encourage the repetition of desired behaviors. Be sure to celebrate successes and say thank you. Focus on finding the good.

Implement an "idea bounty." When implementing a good idea, bestow a twenty-five-dollar gas card on the team member who had the light-bulb moment.

4. Build Autonomy

Autonomy means employees feel trusted to manage their time and energy. Demonstrate that trust by avoiding micromanagement and allowing people to own their work. When possible, let them carry projects from start to finish. Focus on outcomes: define the result you want, then give them space to decide how to achieve it.

Delegate intentionally. Well-matched assignments lead to success, and success builds confidence to take on more responsibility.

Reinforce autonomy by keeping the organization's vision visible. Use images or shared visuals that reflect where the team is headed, and invite employees to contribute. Tie daily work back to that vision.

5. Competition

Gamify the job. A little friendly competition can be a great motivator. (Don't let it get out of hand; however, or you'll see negative results.)

Correlate the steps of a daunting project or the company's most important objectives with milestone rewards. You choose the prize. It can be a button, a badge, or something with monetary value. Give trophies for outstanding performance.

Some experts recommend keeping competitions for teams, not individuals, but it really depends on your group. As a Xennial, I prefer working independently and want my rewards to be such. A mix of individual and group goals may be best. Ensure rules are clear and promote collaboration, not cutthroat competition.

After we've looked at what drives other people, there's an uncomfortable truth: you can't ask others to grow while staying safely unchanged yourself. Motivation has a ceiling when the leader won't take the next step. Chapter 46 shifts from inspiring movement in your team to creating it in your own life, crossing the line where comfort ends and real momentum begins.

CHAPTER 46. GET OUT OF YOUR COMFORT ZONE

Through ambition and persuasive speech, Julius Caesar rose to power as consul and later as governor. In 49 BCE, he was stationed in Ravenna in northern Italy. Publicly, it appeared to be business as usual. After nightfall, however, Caesar made a decisive move: he set out to cross the Rubicon River.

Under Roman law, a governor was forbidden to cross the Rubicon with an army. Doing so was an act of treason, punishable by loss of office and execution.

According to historical accounts, Caesar hesitated. He lost his way in the dark, then found a guide who led him to the riverbank. Gathering nearby soldiers and civilians, Caesar took a trumpet, sounded the signal to advance, and crossed the Rubicon.

That decision led to the fall of the Roman Republic and the rise of the Roman Empire. Caesar later summarized his military success with three words:

Veni, Vidi, Vici

I came, I saw, I conquered.

Know Your Comfort Zone

Comfort is appealing for a reason. It brings a sense of calm and control. When we stay in familiar territory, the brain rewards us with dopamine, serotonin, and endorphins. Working in this zone can be productive, but remaining there limits growth.

Consider what might change if your boundaries were wider. **Most meaningful goals live beyond what feels safe or routine.** Reaching them requires deliberate discomfort.

Outside your comfort zone, anxiety and fear are normal. Stress increases. The brain releases adrenaline and glutamate to prepare for a challenge. These signals aren't signs of failure; they're indicators that you're pushing past what's familiar and moving toward growth.

Test Your Comfort Zone

If you're in a rut, emotionally drained, feeling uninspired, or lacking direction, it's time to test your comfort zone. A good way to test your limits is to track your routine. Write your activities for two weeks. Note any discomfort if you deviate.

Our bodies protect us from harm by sending danger signals when we're in unknown territory. If you feel your heart rate increase, sweat forming, or tension in your body, take note of your specific fears. Which are logical? Which are not?

Fear creates boundaries. Which ones do you need to push to expand your comfort zone? **Decide that you *will* allow yourself a certain measure of discomfort as you break boundaries.**

Benefits of Leaving Your Comfort Zone

Leaving your comfort zone involves risk. But there's also an opportunity. At the extreme, it changes history. At the personal level, it allows you to live out your values more fully. As you move beyond familiar boundaries, your capacity expands. Confidence grows through experience.

I never expected to be a public speaker. At first, I said yes because I needed the work. Over time, something shifted. I wasn't pretending anymore; I was practicing. What once felt forced became natural, and my comfort zone adjusted.

Trying new things builds competence. Experience replaces hesitation. Credibility increases as uncertainty fades.

Your experiences shape how you think, lead, and relate to others. They teach lessons no classroom can replicate. Along the way, you discover new interests, develop meaningful relationships, and gain perspective. Exposure to differences builds empathy and helps you navigate people and situations better.

Get Out of Your Comfort Zone

Follow Caesar's steps to get out of your comfort zone.

1. Shed light. What does it take to get where you want to go? Interview someone who is where you want to be. Do some research. Find an inspiring biography.

2. Outline a path. Start with safe goals. They should be attainable and not too risky. Travel with a guide (mentor) if possible. Check in when you hit an unexpected boulder or fallen tree in your path.

3. Recruit soldiers. Who do you need to help you on your way? It may be a career coach, financial planner, or lawyer. Maybe joining a club or professional organization will help.

4. Announce your intent. Don't just daydream about what could be. You've got a plan; tell the world about it. Gain accountability by shouting it from the riverbank or telling the soldiers you've recruited what you're going to do, how, and when.

5. Cross that Rubicon! You got this!

Stepping outside your comfort zone is rarely dramatic in the moment. More often, it's a series of small, deliberate choices that compound over time. Once you cross your own Rubicon, the question becomes how you sustain that momentum. Chapter 47 focuses on carrying these lessons forward in the long term.

CHAPTER 47. MAKE LONG-TERM CHANGE

Communication is layered, but you've covered a lot of ground in this book. Listening, feedback, boundaries, influence, conflict, and leadership. None of these works in isolation.

The question now isn't *what* you know. It's how you turn what you know into consistent practice. Real change comes from choosing a few behaviors and applying them intentionally, over time.

Start Small and Be Specific

Lasting change is built through focus. Choose one behavior to work on. Not five. Not everything. Maybe it's pausing before responding. Maybe it's naming expectations more clearly. Maybe it's speaking up once when you typically stay quiet.

Work on that one behavior until it becomes automatic. Then move on to the next. Communication skills compound when practiced consistently. If you like structure, use simple if–then planning:

- *If* I feel defensive, *then* I will ask a clarifying question.
- *If* I'm about to send a reactive email, *then* I'll wait ten minutes.

Small decisions, repeated often, create durable habits.

Expect Imperfection

Behavior change isn't linear. You'll revert under stress. That doesn't mean the work isn't sticking; it means you're human. Treat communication like any other professional skill. You don't abandon it because you missed a rep. You notice what happened, adjust, and keep going.

Progress shows up as shorter recovery time, clearer intent, and fewer repeated mistakes, not perfection.

Stay Adaptable

Work changes. Teams change. Life changes. Your communication will feel different under pressure, fatigue, or transition. That's normal. The goal isn't to be flawless; it's to be aware. When something stops working, don't assume failure. Ask:

- What changed?
- What's being asked of me now?
- What needs adjusting?

Strong communicators recalibrate rather than rigidly cling to old patterns.

Check Alignment Regularly

We're often kinder and more thoughtful with customers and strangers than with the people we work with every day. Periodically ask for honest feedback.

- What's helping?
- What's unclear?
- Where am I creating friction without realizing it?

Think of this as a professional "State of the Union." It keeps resentment from building and prevents blind spots from hardening into habits.

Get Support

Change is easier when it's visible. Share your goal with someone you trust. Ask them to notice one specific behavior and give you private feedback. Accountability doesn't need to be formal.

In some cases, additional support can help untangle long-standing patterns. That's not a weakness; it's a strategic choice. Tools work best when the person using them is supported.

Evaluate and Celebrate

Gradual change is easy to miss. That doesn't mean it isn't happening. Pay attention to evidence. Notice when a conversation goes better than it used to, when you pause instead of reacting. When you speak up sooner, or listen longer, than you would have before.

Track progress in a way that works for you. Write it down. Save the email. Accept the compliment without deflecting it. Let success register.

We are wired to remember disappointment more easily than progress. Counteract that tendency intentionally. Some people keep one journal. Others keep two (one for the wins and the other for the struggles). If you choose to keep two journals, don't romanticize the struggle. Learn from what didn't work, then let it go. Don't keep rereading your own mistakes. You've already extracted the lesson. Toss out journal number two, if you'd like.

Make It a Practice

Communication isn't something you "fix." It's something you practice. There will be seasons when you're sharp and seasons when you're tired. Stress will shorten your patience. Pressure will test your habits. That doesn't mean you've failed. It means you're human. Return to the tools. Choose again. Adjust as needed.

Long-term change doesn't come from intensity. It comes from consistency, self-awareness, and the willingness to keep choosing better.

You don't need to master everything in this book. You only need to apply what matters most *right now*. And when that becomes second nature, you'll know exactly what to work on next.

Just keep going.

A FINAL WORD

If this book helped you pause, choose your words more carefully, or approach a difficult conversation with more clarity and confidence, then it's doing its job. The goal was never perfection, only progress. Better conversations lead to better work, stronger relationships, and fewer regrets.

I wrote this book for people who care about how they show up. Leaders with or without titles. Professionals navigating change. Organizations trying to work better together.

If you found value in what you read, I hope I've earned your 5-star review on Amazon or GoodReads.

https://www.amazon.com/dp/1095306715

https://www.goodreads.com/terralfletcher

If you have any other feedback, I welcome you to email me directly at terra@fletcherconsulting.com.

Let's keep the conversation going.

I speak to organizations across industries about communication, leadership, employer branding, and influence, especially during times of change. My sessions are practical, candid, and designed to give people language they can actually use the next day.

If you're looking for a speaker who blends strategy with real-world experience (and skips the clichés), I'd love to connect.

You can also join my newsletter, where I share practical insights, examples from the field, and tools you can apply immediately.

And if social media is your thing, you'll find me there sharing ideas, asking better questions, and occasionally challenging conventional wisdom.

- LinkedIn: https://www.linkedin.com/in/terralfletcher/
- YouTube: https://www.youtube.com/terralfletcher
- Facebook: https://www.facebook.com/fletcherconsulting
- TikTok: https://www.tiktok.com/@terralfletcher

Continue reading

If this book resonated, you may also enjoy my other work. Follow my author page on Amazon for updates.

https://www.amazon.com/author/terralfletcher

ACKNOWLEDGMENTS

Without the support and guidance of these dear souls, this book would not be what it is today. Thank you to my editor, Diana Schramer, my beta readers, Shawano Area Writers, and my husband, Andrew. The support and suggestions of Terry Misfeldt and Wendy Goerl were significant.

I can't leave out my dear grandmother, Vera Drengler. It was she who encouraged me to stand up straight, learn something new every day, and told me not to do anything I wouldn't want on the front page of the newspaper. I can't wait to tell her that I wrote a book.

ABOUT THE AUTHOR

Terra L. Fletcher is a professional speaker, strategist, and author with more than 18 years of experience helping organizations communicate clearly and lead effectively. She has presented hundreds of sessions across industries, translating complex ideas into practical frameworks leaders can use immediately.

Terra was once named Entrepreneur of the Year and is the author of several books. She believes strong communication is built on clarity, respect, and responsibility.

She reads the back of every package, doesn't fast-forward previews, and welcomes typo reports at terra@fletcherconsulting.com

NOTES

1 Wigger, E. (2019). Hostility and Coronary Heart Disease | Unhealthy Work. [online] Unhealthywork.org. Available at: https://unhealthywork.org/psychological-risk-factors/hostility-and-coronary-heart-disease/ [Accessed 12 May 2019].

2 Strunk, William, Jr. The Elements of Style. Harcourt, 1918.

3 "The Provincial Letters." Letter from Blaise Pascal. December 4, 1656.

4 Meyer, Erin. The Culture Map: Breaking through the Invisible Boundaries of Global Business. New York: PublicAffairs, 2014.

5 Johnson, Meagan, and Larry Johnson. Generations, Inc.: From Boomers to Linksters--managing the Friction between Generations at Work. New York: AMACOM, 2010.

6 Deloitte. 2023 Global Gen Z and Millennial Survey: Reshaping the World of Work. New York: Deloitte Global, 2023.
https://www.deloitte.com/global/en/issues/work/genzmillennialsurvey.html

7 Cullen, Maura J. 35 Dumb Things Well-intended People Say: Surprising Things We Say That Widen the Diversity Gap. Garden City, NY: Experts Academy Press, 2008.

8 Empowered Communication – Cascadia Workshops,
http://cascadiaworkshops.com/empowered-communication/ (accessed February 12, 2019).

9 Fisher, Roger, William Ury, and Bruce Patton. Getting to Yes: Negotiating Agreement Without Giving In. Rev. ed. New York: Penguin Books, 2011.

10 Alberti, Robert E., and Michael L. Emmons. Your Perfect Right: Assertiveness and Equality in Your Life and Relationships. 10th ed. San Luis Obispo, CA: Impact Publishers, 2017.

11 McNamara, Carter, MBA, PhD. "Checklist of Categories of Typical Motivators." Free Management Library. Accessed February 12, 2019.
https://managementhelp.org/leadingpeople/motivation-checklist.htm.

www.ingramcontent.com/pod-product-compliance
Lightning Source LLC
Chambersburg PA
CBHW032002170526
45157CB00002B/514